How to sell and market your way
and get your business buzzing l
(even though your customers do

☛ How to **sell** and **market** your way out of this **recession** and get your **business** buzzing like never before

(even though your customers don't want to know)

NICHOLAS **BATE**

infiniteideas

First published in 2009 by
Infinite Ideas Limited
36 St Giles
Oxford, OX1 3LD
United Kingdom
www.infideas.com

A CIP catalogue record for this book is available from the British Library
ISBN 978–1–906821–14–2

Brand and product names are trademarks or registered trademarks of
their respective owners.
Cover designed by Cylinder
Text designed by Baseline Arts Ltd, Oxford
Typeset by Sparks, Oxford – www.sparkspublishing.com
Printed and bound in Britain by TJ International Limited, Cornwall

Mixed Sources

Product group from well-managed
forests and other controlled sources
www.fsc.org   Cert no. SGS-COC-2482
© 1996 Forest Stewardship Council

Contents

Introduction

● ●

Selling is the one and only key to surviving this recession. All else is trivia. Hyperbole? Only a little and you know it, deep down. That's why we've created the very best and latest in thinking and action not just on selling but *specifically on selling in a recession*. If you've never really had to sell before, here's where you'll find out how to do it. If you're usually really great at selling but finding it tough in the current downturn you'll find out how to polish up your skills. And if your team are missing opportunities and giving away profit then that's covered here, too.

It's an incredibly straightforward, really practical guide. We've supplied exact phrases you can adapt for yourself to handle price objections, precise, low-cost, quick-to-implement marketing tactics you can use immediately to flush out those in your market sector who do have budget, and bonus tips if you are trying to squeeze the best performance out of your reduced head-count sales team. Plus all your tough questions are answered in the surgery at the end of each chapter. So specifically, this guide will ensure you are brilliant at:

■ Finding new business;

■ Keeping current business;

■ Handling objections such as 'no budget', 'price too high' and 'didn't you know there is a recession on?';

■ Pitching via email, formal proposal and presentation;

■ Making sure you are unique;

■ Beating the competition;

■ Negotiating, not just giving discount;

■ Getting quality conversations with prospects;

■ Staying profitable;

■ Closing deals on time, in time, to forecast;

■ Staying resilient whatever the pressure.

The book also includes great tips on how to:

■ Motivate your team;

■ Prioritise conflicting opportunities;

■ Create more difference.

Nothing is excluded, to ensure you are extraordinarily good at selling in a recession.

Most importantly the ideas here will be immediately relevant and actionable whether you are running a four-man window-cleaning business, a one-woman consultancy or are responsible for the EMEA quarterly target.

We've structured the book so that the first chapters take you through the essentials of selling in a recession; if you have not done much selling before you'll be fast-tracked. The chapters are designed to get you into the material quickly, with bulleted concepts, all the tricky points fully covered and fast implementable action plans laid out for you. With this part of the book you can dive in and choose the area which is concerning you most, or if the chapters are read in sequence, you'll get a powerful personal workshop.

Chapter 13 gives you a summary so you can ensure you didn't miss anything in the first twelve chapters. Alternatively it can be used for reviewing the ideas with your colleagues or team. Chapter 14 gives you a definitive checklist to ensure you don't lose out on any of the fundamentals of great sales and marketing technique. Chapters 15 and 16 give you more examples of creating that essential difference to your business which, as you will see, is vital to your success. Chapter 17 gives you a step-by-step strategy for implementing the ideas quickly and transforming your business, with Chapter 18 suggesting further resources which you may find useful if you want to dig deeper.

We're completely behind you on this so if you've decided that now is the time to get brilliant at selling – read on.

1. Getting new business

● ●

WHY IS GOING OUT AND PROACTIVELY GETTING NEW BUSINESS SO VITAL?

Look at pretty well any business and notice – understandably, perhaps – how much of their time and energy goes into day-to-day fire-fighting: wrestling contracts out of current customers, resolving problems with long-standing accounts and paying the bills. Frighteningly little measured action is typically taken to find business for next week, next month, next quarter and certainly not next year. When times are buoyant, and, if we're honest, we're only having to answer the phone and take down a credit card number, that strategy is fine. Open the door and magically there will be potential new customers for us to deal with. But sadly in a recession, open the door and there's likely to be nobody there. We've got to get people to our door: regularly and consistently. We need to put time, effort and attention to this critical task and vital skill. So here are ten fast-track ways to do just that.

WHAT YOU NEED TO KNOW: TEN GREAT WAYS TO GET NEW BUSINESS

At any time of the economic cycle, rain or shine, the following are great ways to get new business.

1. Ask when you win business

Every time you win some business, say to your contact, 'Who else should I be talking to?' Both in their business and also generally. Try and get the email address and telephone number of at least one new contact from every won sale. Ask your established contact if you can use them as a reference point to start the new conversation.

2. Ask when you lose business

When you lose business, hopefully your contact will still be in conversation with you and may well value your product: it's just that it wasn't to be this time. So ask them, 'Is there anybody else I could be talking to?' There is nothing to be lost and everything to be gained.

3. Review every sale won

Never assume you know why you won the business! You may think it's because of your price or the fact that you offer it in crimson, but perhaps they actually bought from you because you are local. So ask why they bought from you. You may not get the full story but if you ask enough people you will spot the themes. Turn those themes on their head to identify new business opportunities – businesses which are local to you, perhaps?

4. Ask your current accounts
They're a delightful account. Reliably and happily, they pay the bills and they've been with you for years. You hardly talk business any more. Well now's the time to do so. Find out who they know in the industry. Perhaps there are more opportunities in the account, so ask them. Since the relationship started you my well have developed your business and they may be surprisingly ignorant of all that you do now. It's time to sell to them again.

5. Make it easy to buy
Is your web-site up to date? Can they buy by phone, email and fax? Do you accept a broad range of credit cards? Is your out of hours answerphone message helpful? Is everybody in your business who might speak to a customer sales-trained? Are price lists up to date? When people want 'more information', what do you say and/or provide?

6. Do simple direct marketing
Talk to people who might want to buy from you
Let's just introduce some useful terminology. *Suspects* are people 'out there' who might buy from you. *Prospects* are ones whom you have 'qualified', in other words they do have a need for your product and they have some budget and can make a decision. *Customers* are those who have bought from you. *Clients* are those who have bought regularly. *Advocates* are your top accounts, who rave about you. We've already discussed (see points 1, 3 and 4 above) how to ensure we get the best out of customers, clients and advocates, but how do we talk to our suspects and prospects? By 'marketing' to them, clearly. There's

an important point to make here: a lot of money can be wasted trying to talk to everybody. After all, everybody might use your window-cleaning service. So you could put an insert in the local paper. But actually – your analysis tells you – the majority of your customers are on the east side of town. So maybe a door-to-door leaflet drop promoting that fact, in that area, would be better. In this way you'll be aiming at people who are already a little 'qualified' to do business with you.

What do you say?
You say what will help them. If it's business to business, tell them what will make them more money and help them reduce costs. If it's business to consumer, let them know how you can make their life better or easier in some way. Your messages must pass the 'so what?' test. (There's more on this in Chapter 6, Grabbing business by showing what you can do.) Above all you must give them reasons for talking to you. The mistake too many make, too often, is talking too much about themselves. Your credibility is key – but only after you have grabbed their interest. So a good start might be,

Shiny Windows window-cleaners has an established clientele on the east side of town, which makes it so much easier for you to get your windows cleaned at exactly the times you want … We have been working in your area delighting clients with our perfect professionalism for more than seven years …

What format do you use?

Well, you could just ring people up. That's direct and it does work: we'll be exploring that in a minute. But why not try a simple piece of direct mail, or a door-drop (the idea of course of getting your literature delivered to a local area via, say, a local newspaper). If you want to get more sophisticated you might consider PR, in which case you will probably need some professional help. If you haven't been to any of the exhibitions related to your industry for a while, perhaps now is the time to give one a go.

The key to getting any of these methods to work is to ask, 'What do the people we want to talk to read, look at and listen to? Where do they go at weekends? What are their interests?' You need to grab their attention. You can get clues from your competitors: if one of your successful rivals has been using local radio advertising for two years, that probably works, so you could try that. You could also try something they *don't* do such as an insert in the special business section that comes with the local newspaper. Go where your prospects go, try *something* and measure your results.

7. Do focused telephone cold-calling

Do your research

Before picking up that phone you need:

1. The name of a decision-maker and his/her direct line;

2. A story – a reason for calling;

3. An anticipation of the objections you may well receive, both the classics (I haven't got time) and the specific (that story in the *FT* was inaccurate).

Don't skimp on this research. Look at their web-site, especially the press box; search the internet for the company name and key roles. Ring and speak to various departments. Remember persistence and politeness are a remarkably powerful combination. Forget getting hundreds of names: you want just twenty quality companies with whom you wish to do work.

Plan the call

What will you say? How are they likely to respond? What is your value proposition? Why should they be willing to listen to you? What resistance are they likely to present? As you plan, remember your focus is to get a meeting. That is what you are selling. Thus you will not say,

> *I want to come and talk to you about our company's new cost reduction processes,*

but you might say,

> *I noticed in the* FT *that you are currently going through some reorganisation in order to lower your cost base. I'd love to come and talk about how we might be able to contribute to that, by demonstrating some case studies.*

Introduce yourself: name and company

1. Do this at a steady pace – rushing reveals anxiety and low confidence.

2. Move quickly to ask an open, exploratory question linked specifically to their business. Open questions will encourage them to talk. Exploratory questions signify that you're talking adult to adult. So try something like, '… *and I was wondering, how are you addressing that issue?*'

3. Shut up and handle the resistance. Expect it, and deal with it professionally. Thus when they say, '*I simply don't have time*', you say, '*I wouldn't necessarily expect you to do so now, that's why I would like to set up a meeting…*'. If they say, '*Look, just put something in the post, will you, or email it to me*', you say, '*I'd love to do that but current clients who we approached in this way constantly remind me how it was the face-to-face conversation that revealed the true power of our system/product.*'

4. Close on the meeting: fix a time and date.

5. Thank them.

Do the necessary follow-up actions

For example, write a confirmatory email. Next ask yourself what you could do better next time. Remember:

■ Plan it. Do it. Review it;

■ Politeness + persistence;

■ Expect resistance: anticipate and plan for it;

■ Your goal is the meeting.

Bonus
See chapters on asking questions (Chapter 3), closing (Chapter 7) and handling objections (Chapter 8).

8. Never lose touch with anyone who does business with you
Stay in touch. Try to find reasons – good business reasons – to write to customers and clients at least twice a year. Try and catch them on the phone at least once year. They will buy again one day, and you need to be in the front of their mind when they decide to do so.

9. Measure your results
Don't just throw money at finding new business. One of the few things about a recession is we notice this cost. But the bad thing is we often then switch it off all together: we cannot afford to do that. Know what every bit of marketing costs and what return you get. Emphasise that which works; drop that which doesn't. Eventually you will get to a position that means when you need new business, you can 'turn on the tap' as you know exactly how to get it.

10. Improve what works

Drop what doesn't. Don't do stuff just because you like it or it's fun. Designing creative mailers and hanging out at the agency can be fun. Making cold calls can be hard work. The choice should be about which gets you business.

IN A RECESSION DON'T FORGET THE ABOVE, BUT DO FOCUS ON THESE ESSENTIAL THREE

When things get tough, we can no longer rely on people coming to us or the light-touch ways of getting business. We need to get tougher, more proactive and more focused. Here are the three essentials to remember.

1. Asking

One of the biggest challenges in a recession is the way everybody switches off, shuts down and doesn't want even to talk to you. Hence, if you are in conversation with anybody, make the use of that opportunity. Ask, ask, ask, *'Who else do you know? Who can you introduce me to? Who else on the account ought we to contact?'* Ask for help. They can only say no, and you can cope with that.

2. Focused and selective telephone cold-calling

Make this an essential part of your strategy. It will not be easy, but it will be effective. Identify the wish-list of organisations with whom you want to do work. Do not make assumptions such as, 'Oh, everybody will be trying to contact them.' Yes they may, but by the easy methods not by your chosen focused method. Give yourself a target cold-calling window, say between 9.15 and 11.00, every morning.

3. Creative marketing

Nobody is in any doubt of the wisdom of keeping our names out there when it is tough so that we are poised and ready when times are good again. But making the investment when money is tight can be tricky. So be creative, e.g. instead of spending £500 on lots of ordinary mailers, what about spending £10 per mailer to make individualised and customised mailers for fifteen key target companies. If you've done your research well this is much more likely to get a good return, and if it works you can increase this approach.

EXAMPLES FOR BOOSTING BUSINESS IN THE RECESSION

At Mange-Tout Greengrocers

Why not thank all your regular customers (as you meet them during the week) for their business and give them a simple money-off voucher for the day of the week when you are least busy. Give them one for a friend and ask them to bring someone who doesn't shop with you at the moment. Does it work? Adjust it, try variations until you get it right.

At The Too Pink 'there's no glass ceiling' Consultancy

Why not go back through all the old accounts who have not spent anything with you for 12 months; ring and ask if you can come to tell them what you have been up to recently and introduce your new products, etc. Notice how the first few meetings go. What's working? That's the stuff you want to focus on.

At Intergalactic Software, EMEA Division

Why not create daily cold calling 'blitzes', e.g. for two hours every morning. Get everyone on the phones cold-calling. Create a charged and competitive atmosphere (whooping, high fives, etc.). Offer (small) prizes for caller of the hour. Notice who's having success and work out what they are doing. That's what everyone else should be doing too.

THE SURGERY IS OPEN

We all hate cold-calling. It's not that we don't believe in it: we do; we have over the years got one or two really good bits of business by finally picking up the phone and actually making the call, it's just that ... well ... we all hate it! Are there any ways to make it easier or less painful? For instance, are there any special times of day, special opening lines that always work?

No. There you go: thought I'd say it up front. This book is platitude-free; we promised that. So I could have pretended if you ring at 3pm on a Wednesday afternoon all decision-makers will be receptive. But I don't know. They may be; they may not be. The main thing is for you to ring, to make the call. Making cold calls is hard, but you have all you need to do them well. And bear in mind the anxiety of making a call is a lot less than the anxiety of no business. The more you practise cold-calling, the easier it gets. And in case you missed the earlier subtle point, it'll reach the parts of business your competitors can't get to because they are too frightened to do the calls. There, I knew you would be convinced.

SUMMARY

■ Have a range of methods which ensure your pipeline of business is constantly being topped up.

■ Survey your market of suspects and turn them into prospects.

■ If you can be smart and identify them – immediately – at prospect stage, that will save you a lot of money.

■ Now turn your prospects into paying business, in other words, customers.

■ Try the methods which many people forget, such as simply asking!

■ Try the methods which many – being honest – are frightened of attempting, such as cold-calling.

THINGS TO DO

1. Identify methods you do know how to use, but which have fallen into disuse. Give someone in your business responsibility for re-vitalising those methods.

2. Identify methods which you haven't been using. Give someone responsibility to action them. (See Chapter 4, Practise, practise, practise.)

3. Start noting which methods really, really work for you. Refine them for better overall pay-off (i.e. more business won for less spend).

4. **Start today.**

2. Qualifying, prioritising and tracking new business

WHY IS QUALIFYING, PRIORITISING AND TRACKING YOUR
NEW BUSINESS SO VITAL?

Although at some of the worst points of the recession – when the
phone isn't ringing, there are no email enquires and you are lost for
inspiration as to where next to seek new business – it can seem that
you have plenty of time. However, that should not be the case for
long if you are following through on these ideas. A basic strategy
is that you must maximise PCT (that's prospect contact time) and
CCT (that's customer contact time). That's where your life-blood
revenue starts. Every bit of looking for and trying to win business is
not only a potential opportunity to earn revenue and profit but also
a potential liability in that it can suck up time which you could be

spending on other selling activities, such as a better quality prospect. Be careful not to be driven by simple urgency, apparent large budgets or desperation. So you need to qualify (could it actually become business?) and prioritise (who do I deal with first?). You also need to track (what's the next stage with that client I spoke to last week?). For most of us, our sales go through various stages: pitches, negotiations, meeting new decision-makers, proposals, new proposals. We need to always be on track of the next step. Here's how you can achieve that.

WHAT YOU NEED TO KNOW: TEN GREAT WAYS TO QUALIFY, PRIORITISE AND TRACK NEW BUSINESS

At any time of the economic cycle, rain or shine, the following are great ways to qualify, track and prioritise new business.

1. Qualify by asking about budget

Early on, you need to find out whether the decision-maker you are speaking to has any money to spend, and if so, how much. Sometimes people are embarrassed to ask these questions. Don't be: you can't do your job if you don't know their budget and you may be wasting your time if they have none. Thus when selling in a clothing shop you might ask, *'How much were you thinking of spending on your jeans?'*; if you're working in an advertising agency you might say to the client, *'There are various ways we can handle this campaign. Clearly you want to do it cost-effectively, so what sort of budget do you have in mind?'*

2. Qualify by asking about decision-making capability

Don't accept a 'no' from somebody who can't give you a 'yes'. You need to be talking to the person who makes the decisions. Be firm. Your time is money. Don't be messed about. Ask to talk to those who make the decisions and insist they are at important meetings. So try something like, '*I know she's busy but it is essential that she be at the first meeting so we know everything accurately, including the budget options.*'

3. Qualify by asking about their need

Don't assume someone is thinking of buying simply because they are talking to you. Or buying now. They may just be interested, they may be using you to compare online prices. Find out what they need. If you're behind the counter in a camera shop ask, 'What particularly brings you in here today, how can we help you?'

4. Prioritise by deciding what's important to you

If you implement all the ideas from this book, you'll soon have too many potential possibilities. While that's great news, you'll need to decide which get most and which get least attention – you need to put your prospects in order. Ah, but against what criteria? That depends on several factors. For example, if business is very, very difficult for you at the moment, you may want to prioritise by quick easy wins, just to get cash in. Or maybe those easy wins are coming in and that's the problem; they are not profitable and not growing your business. So you may want to prioritise by much harder but longer term strategic wins. A sale can bring you revenue, profit, market-share, PR prestige or even take you into a new market area. Decide what you want and 'sort' by that.

5. Prioritise by having a simple system

Once you have decided your prioritisation factors, ensure every bit of business is sorted by that. A matrix on the white-board may be enough, or maybe a spreadsheet is needed – just be sure to keep it really simple.

6. Track by deciding the essential stages

Ensure you know what stages your sales go through. In a consultancy it might be initial enquiry ➔ qualification ➔ pitch 1 ➔ pitch 2 ➔ proposal, and so on. With a window-cleaning business it might be a door drop ➔ take initial booking ➔ follow-up for regular booking. Decide all the important stages.

7. Track by creating a simple system

Now combine your priorities system with your tracking system. Again. It could be a matrix on the white-board. Top to bottom, highest to lowest priority. Scanning along horizontally, you'll be able to see what stage of the sales cycle you are at. If you are a window-cleaner, you might be able to do it on the back of an envelope. If you are a large firm of accountants, you probably need a simple spreadsheet. But in any case you need a system.

8. Qualify, prioritise and track by teaching everyone how to use the process

Insist that opportunities are not held solely in the head. It's true that the current and/or number one of most opportunities will be remembered successfully, but all the lesser ones which need progressing can be forgotten easily. That's when clients get angry and/or competition comes in. Either way you lose the business.

9. Qualify, prioritise and track by reviewing and improving

Don't simply throw money at finding new business. In a recession we really notice our marketing costs. But the bad thing is we often then switch them off altogether: we cannot afford to do that. Knowing what every bit of marketing costs and what return you get is vital – this tracking system allows you to do that.

10. Use the results as simple market research data

Once you have been using this system for a few weeks you'll be able to spot some patterns and see answers to questions such as, 'Where does our quality business come from?', 'Which is our most profitable business?', 'When do we seem to be able to close easily?' Once you have some answers link this information back to Chapter 1, Getting new business.

IN A RECESSION DON'T FORGET THE ABOVE, BUT DO FOCUS ON THESE ESSENTIAL FOUR

When things get tough, we can no longer rely on there being another bit of business to fill the gap if we lose a deal or two. We must be on top of every sale and give it the attention it needs to win it.

1. Qualification

There are three important factors regarding qualification in a recession. First, the ground will be shifting rapidly. Even your decision-maker may not know that his or her budget has just been removed. So qualify and requalify every meeting and every call (*'So can I just check that we are still looking at a spend of 315k?'*). Second, your more naive decision-makers will be out of their depth and assume that just as when business was buoyant they'll find the money they need. You know that this is no longer the case. Ask politely and persistently where the funds are, and check the spend has been approved as necessary. Third, you'll meet good accounts and decision-makers with no money. Don't ditch them, because their day will come. Get them on your tracking system and stay in touch: find out when their next financial year starts.

2. Prioritisation

In a recession, it's important to be pragmatic. For most businesses, quick results are vital. So make that your choice and don't be distracted. Once you've got cash coming in, start building for the thaw; it will come. Which accounts can grow your business and market share?

3. Use the system

Not using the system doesn't just mean you lose business. It means you don't know how much business you are losing. It's the latter which is most frightening.

4. Get everyone using the system

Get everyone using the system, not only so that you know resources are being used wisely but also so that if anyone is ill or leaves, the account can be picked up immediately.

EXAMPLES FOR BOOSTING BUSINESS IN THE RECESSION

At Inside-Out Gentleman's Tailor

Why not realise that 'stage 1' for most of your potential new customers is the 'just looking and comparing versus other upmarket tailors' stage. What can you do in that stage 1 to distinguish yourself? Perhaps you could offer a free (quality) coffee and a sit-down chat at a small table to one side of the shop? Talk to them about what they are looking for, find out whether they have bought bespoke clothing before, and so on.

At The Too Pink 'there's no glass ceiling' Consultancy

Why not firstly decide what is vital at the moment? Be pragmatic: are you desperate for cash to keep the bank manager at bay? OK: then that's what you focus on. In six months' time, you can use another criterion such as profitability. But for now, focus on what you want and need.

At Intergalactic Software, EMEA Division

Why not do a total account review? Which ones will be spending this financial year? Are you giving them the TLC and attention they need? Do not prioritise attention by who shouts the loudest but by potential. Do not prioritise by who is nice to have lunch with but who will support the growth of your business. Be willing to reassign priorities. Last year they were an A account, maybe this year they are a D account. The system needs to be simple, pragmatic and used.

THE SURGERY IS OPEN

I know I need to qualify. I've seen the disastrous consequences of not doing so: months of time and energy wasted. I even once learnt a mnemonic: M-A-N: money, authority, need. But putting it bluntly: prospects sometimes lie for negotiation reasons or won't tell us their criteria. So, what do we do?

You are right. There are a range of reasons why you can't get the information you need to do your job: some contacts misinform us because of a misguided feeling that it will help them when it comes to negotiating a good deal. Naivety sometimes plays a part, too. Who knows why people do it? But one thing is for sure: if you keep asking questions at your meetings and during your calls and if you keep asking those same questions of different people: you will get the precise information you need. Accuracy's always 'outed' by repeated probing. Ask about budget, ask about who decides. Keep checking what they really want.

SUMMARY

- Boost PCT (prospect contact time) and CCT (customer contact time).

- Develop a range of questions and approaches which allows you to qualify all business, early in your sales cycle. Without that you could be spending time with the wrong prospect or totally wasting time.

▪ Create a simple system, using your current 'desirable business' criteria, which will allow you to match your valuable selling resource against the business you truly want.

▪ Ensure your system is sufficiently simple that: 1. All understand it, 2. All use it, 3. All value it.

THINGS TO DO

1. Start qualifying all business. Today.

2. Start prioritising all business. Today.

3. Create a simple system – which all those involved with the sales process are committed to using – which allows the tracking of all sales from initial qualification to won or 'closed'. Tomorrow.

4. Start noting which methods of selling really, really work for you: your tracking process will give feedback on this. Refine processes for better overall pay-off (i.e. more business won for less spend). Today plus seven days.

5. **Start today**.

3. Asking questions

● ●

WHY IS ASKING QUESTIONS SO VITAL?

The question is your selling power tool. A question gets someone to stop and think. When you ask someone a question, they have to give you attention. Asking a question can allow you to direct attention to a relevant point. Asking a question can make an issue smaller or larger, it can influence someone's thinking. Above all we live in a world of 'tell' – especially the sales world. So when you ask key, strategic questions you become different; you start distinguishing yourself from your competitors. You wake your customer up to the issues they need to consider rather than sending them into another trance-inducing PowerPoint tell, tell, tell, haphazard, hope-for-the-best pitch. And, well, you'll notice you start winning the business, especially if you follow the hints below.

WHAT YOU NEED TO KNOW: TEN GREAT WAYS TO USE QUESTIONS TO WIN BUSINESS

At any time of the economic cycle, rain or shine, these are powerful ways to use questions to gain new business.

1. Realise you have a portfolio of three question types: open, closed and pain

You once read a book about selling at an airport when you were delayed because of fog. Yep, that's right, you have some dim memories:

something about 'open and closed questions'. Open questions (involving words like what, why, how, where, when, who) tend to encourage someone to talk. They're great for starting conversations and getting loads of information. What's the background to this project? How will you decide? What are the key issues for you? What are you looking for in a new flat? They are poor for pinning things down, though. That's where closed questions come in: Will you personally be deciding on the supplier? What exactly is the new budget? These have a definite 'yes' or 'no' answer, or a finite one-word answer. They are brilliant for discovering next steps, making agreements and so on. And then there are 'pain questions'. These make an issue more important, perhaps one that you are encouraging the prospect to take more seriously. For example, when selling your new software package: *'And what is the cost to you of not having an accurate daily report of items sold by shop?'* Or as a heating engineer you might try: *'I agree that the service contract seems an additional expense now, but what happens if your boiler breaks down?'*

2. Use questions to build rapport

How was your journey? How long have you been working here? Just chatty stuff to help you get into the main conversation. Open questions are perfect here.

3. Use questions to qualify the business

So what is your budget? And will anybody else be involved in the decision? (Go back and look at Chapter 2 if you're not sure.)

4. Use questions to influence the buying criteria

They say they want to work with a big company. You're a small company. So probe: what's the attraction of working with a big company? They might say that excellent, rapid support is essential. So you say, '*Ahh, so support is the big issue for you? Let me explain our excellent customer support package.*' Good work: you used questions to influence from a 'big company' criterion which you couldn't provide to 'excellent customer support', which you can.

5. Use questions to make an issue more important

When you notice an issue which matches one of your strengths, build the issue. He is buying a roller-bag. You notice him mention several times how much international travel he does. Ask how many trips he does, how often he uses his bag. This will all help reinforce in his mind that he is making a sensible investment in your (pricey) quality bag.

6. Use questions to direct the prospect's attention

The event manager is considering your conference centre amongst others. You have beautiful grounds but she's ignoring that fact despite your 'tell' hints. So, ask, '*How do you keep your delegates energised during the day?*' Then remind her that brisk walks at breaks in your beautiful grounds can be wonderfully reinvigorating. Much better than being off a roundabout on the 'accessible M4'.

7. Use questions to agree a next stage

So, what do you see as the next stage? Do we agree that I will come and present to your board next Thursday at ten? So you will take clothing samples and let us have feedback by 1 October?

8. Use questions to ask for leads

Is there anyone else I could be speaking to about this new upgrade? Thank you so much. And may I mention your name? Great: I appreciate that.

9. Use questions to give you thinking time

While they are answering, listen to their answer but also think about where you want to go next. Open it up again: *'Can you tell me more about that?'* Or focus in: *'So what exactly would that mean: in a word or two?'* Maybe you want them to really think about that issue: *'And the implication of not being able to do that would be …?'*

10. Use questions to get account feedback

'On a scale of 1 to 10 how happy are you with our approach and performance? … Oh, that's kind: 8½. What would we need to do to get a 10?'

'And of these three very valuable suggestions, which would you say is the most important? … Interesting, thank you.'

IN A RECESSION DON'T FORGET THE ABOVE, BUT DO FOCUS ON THESE ESSENTIAL SIX

When things get tough and money is tighter, budgets can disappear overnight and the competion can play dirty. We can use questions to pre-handle all of these issues.

1. Make an issue more important

In a recession, many markets shrink, budgets slip away. Know your USPs (unique selling points), the things that are special about you and make you stand out from the crowd, and ensure you get them across (see Chapter 6 for more on this). You can do this by telling, '*We are the number 1 producer of this in Western Europe*', or you can ask, '*How important is the supply chain to you?*' The latter will take a few minutes longer but it is selling rather than telling.

2. Changing criteria

Prospects buy against criteria, but are they your criteria? Ensure more of the money out there comes to you. So they want a pink dress and you don't have any in stock. Change the criteria by asking questions. You say, '*May I ask why you were keen on pink?*' They respond, '*I wanted to make a real impact at the party.*' You say, '*Well although we don't have pink, we do have some fabulous dresses which will certainly cause heads to turn. Let's take a look.*' Ask don't tell – sell don't tell.

3. Check that accounts are OK

If you have an account which has money and is buying, the competition are certainly going to try and get into your account. If you are selling into a sector which has budget, the competition are going to try and grab a slice. Find out early about account unhappiness by asking and solving the problem. Don't wait until you've lost the account.

4. Keep closing

Business is extremely volatile in a recession so don't lose any by not knowing what the next stage is. '*So, when will we be able to expect a decision? ... What would be the next best step for both of us?*'

5. Ask for other opportunities

There is always some more business in any account. And even if it's a small amount, it's well worth having if you are already in the business. See if you can get it by asking questions like, '*Who should I be talking to?*' or '*Who normally does your budget round?*'

6. Take better notes

Don't try to write everything down. Split your pad with a vertical line two-thirds of the way across the page. On the left, jot down points, charts, needs and issues. But on the right, put action points: this enables a rapid summary at any time.

EXAMPLES FOR BOOSTING BUSINESS IN THE RECESSION

At Mange-Tout Greengrocers

As well as asking all your customers the simple question of 'How are you today?', why not also ask them what else could we – the greengrocer, that is – be providing for you? For example, 'Ahh, Mrs Smith. Wonderful day, isn't it? So good to see you again. I see you like our bananas and grapes; what else could we be providing in our fruit range?' Look for common themes.

At The Too Pink 'there's no glass ceiling' Consultancy

Why not ask questions which reveal the problems your clients will have if they deal with a consultancy that neither understands nor has any passion for the women's market. For example, *'What first attracted you to talking to a consultancy which specialises in the women's market? What do you see as the challenge of consultants who don't really have a connection with many of the challenges facing high-performing women in male dominated organisations?'*

At Intergalactic Software, EMEA Division

Why not ensure everybody asks the decision-making capability of every caller. For example, *'And Tom, may I just ask you: will you be deciding the budget on this project? ... No, I understand that, so who does?'*

THE SURGERY IS OPEN

Isn't a bit direct, even rude, to ask 'pain' questions of someone and his/her business?

It's only rude if:

1.   You haven't developed a bit of rapport, which you will do (be interested in them and their business, be polite, be friendly);

2.   You haven't earned the right to ask powerful questions, which you will do (be professional, show that you are adding value, lead up to these powerful questions);

3.   Your tone is rude, which it won't be.

As long as you remember these three points, your pain questions will really get the prospect thinking. So spend time developing rapport and understanding their business; try and keep your questions flowing and conversational rather than becoming an interrogation. Take care with too much use of 'Why?' – build up to such powerful questions so they realise you are on their side and you do know what they are talking about. When the prospect is ready ask those 'crunch' questions gently: *'So, finally may I ask what happens if this campaign you are looking to do simply doesn't connect with the correct people?'* Ahhh. Now you've got them.

SUMMARY

■ Careful: we have become a tell world.

■ Tell is attractive, tell is easy.

■ Too much tell, especially too much PowerPoint, can just create another 'me-too', trance-inducing presentation and/or conversation.

■ Our goal is to really connect with our prospect and do that rapidly.

■ Without a connection, people aren't really listening and certainly not being influenced.

■ Ask questions to inform, influence, inspire and agree action.

■ We do need to tell at some stage.

■ Telling comes later, once we have done plenty of asking.

■ Get good at open, closed and pain questions.

THINGS TO DO

1   Set up some simple role-plays during your team meetings. This is the area of selling to practise, practise, practise. Chapter 5 will help with setting up these practice sessions.

2   Create a list of clever, powerful questions which strengthen the reasons for choosing your products in your typical selling scenarios. Get them onto index cards, laminate them and give them to all the sales team. Test them regularly!

3   Start noting which methods really, really work for you. Which questions really, really get to the heart of the matter? Refine them for better overall pay-off (i.e. more business won for less spend and/or time). Update the index cards. Reissue. Re-test. Rehearse.

4   **Start today**.

4. Practise, practise, practise

● ●

WHY IS PRACTICE IN THE SELLING GAME SO VITAL?

We'd be outraged if our favourite football team lost a game and we then heard they hadn't bothered to practise; we'd be stunned if our favoured tennis player said he wasn't going to attend training sessions any more because he claimed he knew all there was to know about the game. What about if our favourite actress hadn't learnt her lines before going on stage? Or if a top band hadn't done some rehearsal gigs before the world tour?

Name any field, and the best, well: they practise. They go to training, they rehearse. It's just simply what you do if you want to be good, to be brilliant.

Er … except the world of commerce? Odd that, isn't it? We rarely use part of team meetings to, say, practise good questions, presentations or objection-handling. We don't pretend to be the competition and sell passionately as if we were them and get our colleagues to pull us apart. In short we don't practise, attend training, rehearse or read enough about selling, and it's a shame because it's the real difference that can make the difference. Practising your pitch and technique is vital in a recession because opportunities to win are so greatly reduced to begin with. So read on and learn how through practice you can greatly improve your performance.

WHAT YOU NEED TO KNOW: TEN GREAT WAYS TO PRACTISE

At any time of the economic cycle, rain or shine, these are great ways to practise your essential sales skills.

1. Practise at team meetings

Team meetings often become a transfer of 'admin' information. Even the sharing of sales figures often involves too many people. Go right back to basics and decide what your team meetings are about. They should certainly be about inspiration and development. Well-managed practice sessions can be an excellent part of that.

2. Practise during training sessions

All training should contain very practical elements. Work with your product teams to ensure that occurs. Don't just tell, or present Power-Point decks, but practise, too.

3. Practise on the way to the call

If you are on your own, articulate phrases you might use in your head. If you are driving with a colleague, talk through the conversation.

4. Practise by indentifying a clear skill

For example, practise open questions. Explain what is wanted: demonstrate a good example, demonstrate a bad example. Then get people into threes: one selling, one being the client and one observing. Move the session around every five minutes. Keep it fast and furious with plenty of feedback.

5. Practise by catching people doing things right

Too many development sessions are demoralising. Focus on what is working and get people to build upon that. Once you have that positive environment you can notice what is working less well and start adjusting without resentment from the team.

6. Practise questions

Ensure people can use all three types of question: open, closed and pain.

7. Practise presentations

Ensure people use the seven-part structure (see Chapter 6 for the detail on this).

8. Practise closing

Ensure your sales people are closing and are capable of handling objections (see Chapters 7 and 8 respectively for more detail on this).

9. Measure your results

Which training sessions really work? Focus on this type of session ond do more like that.

10. Improve what works

Make the role-plays even tougher. Produce better product benefit notes. Schedule them more frequently.

IN A RECESSION DON'T FORGET THE ABOVE, BUT DO FOCUS ON THESE ESSENTIAL SIX

When things get tough, we can't afford to let real or live events be our rehearsals. We must practise when there is nothing to be lost but our time and patience (and perhaps ego). Focus on the six elements below.

1. Qualifying

One of the biggest challenges in a recession is that everybody switches off, shuts down and doesn't want to even talk to you. Make every call, every question, every conversation count by proper money/authority/need practise.

2. Focused and selective telephone cold-calling

There's no doubt that this is a tough skill to develop. But it's a very high pay-off skill for those who get good at it. Practise, practise, practise. Who gets good results? What specifically do they do? Replicate their approach across the team.

3. Objection-handling

Assuming qualification has been done well, poor objection-handling can potentially lose the sale. Make sure objections about everything, from price to function, can be handled professionally. At every team meeting, ask the question, 'What objections are we facing?' List objections and resolve them.

4. Closing
Practice instils confidence in a skill which is less about technique and more about self-confidence.

5. Negotiation
If you are not going to give away all your profit you need to practise this gentle art. Anticipate and prepare for that awful question, '*And if we do go ahead, how much discount will you be giving us?*'

6. Playback
Do not do this immediately, but once the team has had plenty of basic practice, start using a video camera to record the role-plays, and play back strong and weak parts. Play the strong parts to build their confidence and encourage them to do more and use the weak parts to make suggestions (not to focus on individual weaknesses).

EXAMPLES FOR BOOSTING BUSINESS IN THE RECESSION

At Just-too-Smart Gent's Hairdresser
Why not read a book on running a small business? Just one good idea would pay for the book. Learn how to up-sell: '*And would you like to take some of our hair-gel with you?*', or cross-sell: '*My colleague has just opened a men's spa – here's a voucher for a discounted manicure.*'

At The Too Pink 'there's no glass ceiling' Consultancy
Why not arrange a half-day off-site workshop for you and your colleagues to practise your 'Why us?' story? Do it a couple of times, then invite a friendly client to come and critique it.

At Intergalactic Software, EMEA Division

Why not arrange an ongoing training programme for leaders on how to coach their staff?

THE SURGERY IS OPEN

Don't get me wrong. I believe in training, but whenever we arrange any or put practice on the team meeting agenda, it gets cancelled or squeezed out. Isn't that just the reality?

No! It's your reality. You say you believe in training? Then don't let it be cancelled! Notice the powerful difference it makes, and then it won't be cancelled or squeezed out in the future. You're there to sell or get better at selling. All that other stuff is getting in the way. Reassert the correct priorities!

Remember to stress to the team that all the people they admire became good at their jobs by practising and that that's all this is about. The mistakes need to happen in the safety of the office: not in the client's office. And if they feel nervous or even embarrassed about doing role-plays in front of their colleagues, well, frankly that's tough. After a couple of sessions that fear will be lost. Guaranteed.

SUMMARY

■ Make practising essential sales skills a bigger part of your team meetings.

■ Arrange more sales training for you and your team.

■ Buy good sales books and circulate them.

■ Reward managers who focus on practice and get it to work.

■ Land heavily on those who don't practise their skills.

THINGS TO DO

1. Book your first practice session for the next team meeting. Today.

2. Arrange a training course. Today.

3. Start noting which methods really, really work for you. Refine them for better overall pay-off (i.e. more business won for less spend/time on practice).

4. **Start today.**

5. Understanding, developing and locking-in the business

● ●

WHY IS UNDERSTANDING, DEVELOPING AND LOCKING-IN THE BUSINESS SO VITAL?

You have done a fantastic job so far. You've found business, no easy feat in a recession, and you've qualified it. Excellent. So now your job really starts: you need to find out what they really want from you and both show them you can do it and keep out the competition. That latter point is vital. Unless you are very lucky you do not have a unique product. And if you do, somebody is copying you at this very moment! No, it is a rare person or company that has a truly unique offering. There is (nearly) always another garage, clothes shop, café, consultancy, software company your prospects could go to. But you are not going to let them!

This is a subtle point, lost on many. Selling is not telling. Or rather it should only be a small amount of confirmatory telling. Marketing does telling, which we hope gives us the introduction. The flyer got them to ring you up. But now with selling you need to convince them, for example, that you are the perfect history tutor for their son. And you do this by:

■ Asking: *'So what are the main difficulties he is having with the subject?'*;

■ Understanding: *'So it's more about learning the facts than understanding the concepts?'*;

■ Listening: *'Yes, do give a few more examples'*;

■ Influencing: *'How about if I started with a verbal test?'*

In this way you get them to realise that you are the one and only solution for them.

WHAT YOU NEED TO KNOW: TEN GREAT WAYS TO UNDERSTAND, DEVELOP AND LOCK-IN THE BUSINESS

At any time of the economic cycle, rain or shine, these are great ways to ensure you not only get but also *don't lose* the business.

1. Understand by finding out what they really want

Not just a haircut, but to look younger. Not just financial planning software, but to reduce costs. When you show that you understand what they really want, you are valued for that skill in itself but you can also offer a full solution rather than a partial one. Hence the importance of asking questions.

2. Understand by listening

The better you know your product, the more dangerous the assumption becomes: 'I know what this prospect wants.' They may not actually want the cheapest insurance; maybe they want the most comprehensive. So listen.

3. Understand by taking notes

The more comprehensive the solution we offer, the easier we can forget the details of our meeting. Write down essential points: *'So what's most important about the house extension you are planning with us?'* Write it down!

4. Develop through open questions

Encourage them to talk with open questions: really understand what they want. Discover other issues, deeper opportunities: *'So, what would be an ideal outcome for you? ... That's very helpful: tell me a little more about your retirement plans.'* Let them talk.

5. Develop through closed questions

Get precision: *'So could you put those four needs in priority order, please?'*, *'And if it were not possible to get an investment which were both high growth and very secure, which option would you personally choose?'*

6. Develop through pain questions

'And if I may pursue this point, what will happen if you don't get the level of reporting you are looking for?','I agree this dental work can seem expensive, but what might happen long-term if the problem is not treated?'

7. Lock in with USPs

USPs are unique selling points, the things you do differently. Maybe you come in red, maybe you act internationally or maybe you're local with a 30 minute response time. It doesn't really matter too much as long as you are different and the difference adds value. If the prospect wants your difference, you're made. Which should remind you that part of this needs-identification process is to influence so that they do want what you offer. Stage one is your USP list. There are three potential kinds:

■ Company: what does your company do differently?

■ Product: what does the product do differently?

■ You: and what's special about you?

Once you know your USPs, stage two is to make sure they are valued by the prospect. You can do that by telling or by asking, but the latter is a lot more powerful because the prospect has 'self-realised' it, rather than been told. Compare:

'So, we are an international company with offices in London, New York, Singapore, Paris and Sydney'.

with

> *'May I ask about your growth plans?'*

(They talk about their ambitious international growth plans.)

> *'So having a model which can be rolled out worldwide without significant extra cost would be helpful then? Let me tell you about our international network …'*

8. Understand that the personal USP is delivering excellence

Unless you are a one-man band, or you have very fast communication and R&D lines, you have little control over company and product USPs; but you do have full control over the third element – you. So make that your priority. Be superb: excel at what you do. People like dealing with excellent people.

9. Lock in with urgency

You will be selling benefits (more of these in Chapter 6). Benefits encourage someone to act because they reveal what they will get as a result of buying. Reassurance and peace of mind with the insurance policy, more room for the children with the extension. But sometimes benefits are not enough: we need to remind the prospect of the cost of not going ahead, e.g. the risk of a director ending up in court with expensive costs if they don't buy the insurance policy.

10. Know the competion's USPs

To position yourself against their USPs, you must know them. A fast way to this information is, whenever you win or lose business, to ask the prospect/customer what was being offered on both sides. They may or may not tell you, but most will.

IN A RECESSION: DON'T FORGET THE ABOVE, BUT DO FOCUS ON THESE ESSENTIAL THREE

When things get tough, there are three keys in this part of the sales process.

1. Differentiation

In a downturn, there are too many suppliers, so you need to be **the one**. You do that by proving you are special. Keep brainstorming what's special about you. Keep creating and trialling ideas to distinguish yourself. No difference: you are a commodity. If you are a commodity, you are selling on price. And unless you are selling huge volume and have significant buying power, the strategy of selling solely on price will probably fail. Ouch.

2. Investment not cost

In a recession people want to delete cost from their spreadsheets. Bottled water? Out! Consultant? Out! Fifty per cent of the work-force? Out! You must show that what you offer is an investment. The coffee machine is an investment in employee morale during a tough working day. The training you offer is an incremental improvement in maximising the best from the best people in your organisation.

3. Urgency

Don't just sell your product. Sell action. A sale made and then deferred until the next quarter is – in a recession – effectively lost. Build urgency into your story: why must they act now? There are two vital messages here: the benefits of action now, and the cost of not going ahead.

EXAMPLES FOR BOOSTING BUSINESS IN THE RECESSION

At Mange-Tout Greengrocers

Why not put up a different poster every week reminding customers what's special about you: organic, local, established for 45 years, etc. But keep changing the sign so that people keep noticing it. Are there any that people remark on – that clearly are particularly important to them?

At The Too Pink 'there's no glass ceiling' Consultancy

You've begun to assume that everyone knows and understands your main USP: deep understanding of and rapport with the women's market. Why not give some real explanation in your brochure – less qualitative, more quantitative?

At Intergalactic Software, EMEA Division

Why not emphasise the personal qualities which are so often lost in large organisations? Think globally, but act locally. If you get it right: a winning combination.

THE SURGERY IS OPEN

I hate to admit to this, but we sell a commodity – essentially we are in the stationery market – and have always sold on price. In boom times we weren't always the cheapest but were cheap enough. Now that the market has shrunk, we are not cheap enough across a wide enough range and we are losing business. So what do we do? We have no USPs.

You do. Let's accept that on company and product you are the same as everybody else. However, you have a bunch of people: those in the warehouse, those answering the phone, those at reception etc. Those people can be OK or good or excellent under your leadership. You can train and inspire them to be excellent. And after all, as there is a diminishing jobs market, they should be happy to take part in this personal development. However cheap a product is, people still want proper service: reams of paper need to get there on time in perfect condition. Water coolers need servicing. People need to pay cheques in at lunchtime and it's nicer if the person is friendly. You get the idea. Get your people to do what they do and do it brilliantly. Then you won't have to be the cheapest: word will spread and if, as you say, you are cheap enough, they will still choose you.

SUMMARY

■ Ensure all business identified and qualified is then developed properly by firstly understanding what the prospect wants.

■ Develop those needs to match well to your USPs.

■ Lock business into you, through demonstrating a need for your USPs.

■ Create a real sense of urgency.

■ Know your USPs for the company, the product and you.

■ Know your competitor's company and product USPs.

THINGS TO DO

1. Add to your pack of laminated index cards those which list company and product USPs.

2. Ensure everyone practises repeatedly the skill of 'understanding, developing and locking-in' the prospect's needs.

3. Train everybody so they excel at what they do, a clear winning personal USP.

4. Allocate one competitor to each of the sales team. Ask your team member to understand how this competitor sells and what their strengths and weaknesses are. Create a card which is added to the pack summarising the information.

5. **Start today.**

6. Grabbing business by showing what you can do

● ●

WHY IS GRABBING THE BUSINESS SO VITAL?

You have found potential business and qualified it as being real. You have influenced the buyer so their preference is you: now you need to show them you can do it! Should be easy? Well, sort of. You have done so much of the hard work up front, that's true – but a few factors are at play. One important one is that as the prospect gets closer to the final decision of 'I will buy', they often also begin to worry, 'Is this the right decision?', 'Are there other possibilities out there?' Such feelings and thoughts are natural so you must learn to manage them. The second important factor is that if the competition are anything like as good as you, they will not give up. So you need to show the prospect you can do it, maintain momentum and keep out the competition. Follow the ideas below.

WHAT YOU NEED TO KNOW: TEN GREAT WAYS TO SHOW THEM YOU CAN DO IT

At any time of the economic cycle, rain or shine, these are great ways to move towards confirming that the business is yours.

1. Clearly explain your solution by answering every one of their points

Whether it is in conversation, via email or at a big pitch, answer everyone of their points fully. A prospect mentions a point because it's important to them. It doesn't mean you can't influence it, but definitely answer it and show respect for the point; ignore it and it might go away, but it's unlikely. So you say, '*You're right, these jeans are a bit more pricey, but they are a classic style which will outlast fads and trends so they are really worth the investment.*'

2. Be enthusiastic

Show that you want the business and that you want to work with them. Enthusiasm really does breed enthusiasm. People like to work with upbeat people.

3. Use all the senses to sell

People actually buy with all of them. We tend to overly concentrate on the visual: the written word or the PowerPoint pitch. But that small, too-hot meeting room with a broken printer in the corner reeks of unprofessionalism: it just doesn't stack up with the words of excellence in the brochure does it? What does the quality of your coffee imply? Or that you turned up in jeans 'because you can sort of get away with it'. Mmm, something to think about.

4. Use clear email

Email does not excuse a poor approach. Structure it:

■ Have a clear subject line;

■ Summarise the situation so far and explain why you are writing;

■ Iterate your points, clearly laid out, numbered in a list if at all possible for ease of reading and access;

■ Summarise;

■ Be clear about what you want them to do.

5. Use a clear proposal

Again, use a structure, but draw out a strong executive summary: remember that many on the circulation list for your proposal will just scan it. That summary can help sell it. So your structure will probably be:

■ Executive summary;

■ Their needs;

■ How you can provide a solution;

■ Costs/fees;

■ Action steps, plus appendices such as product details, company background etc.

6. Use a presentation or pitch

The more complex the sale, the greater the number of decision-makers in the room, the more discussion there is likely to be: these are all good reasons for doing a presentation. But the presentation should be specific to what they want, not a generic pitch where we hope and see what happens. And please read this bit very carefully: *remember that the only reason you gather people in a room and present to them is so that you can, collectively, get their action.* If you don't want action, then just send an email. Presentations are powerful: they should add focus and momentum, all of which can get you want you want.

Don't use PowerPoint badly. There is nothing inherently 'bad' about PowerPoint; it's the poor use of PowerPoint which is the problem. Here are the top poor uses:

■ Script on a slide. It is very easy to write your presentation directly onto PowerPoint; the consequence of this is that many people end up presenting their notes or script. Write your presentation first. Then decide if and how many slides you need.

■ Busy, busy, busy. Busy does not equate to extra value; it simply causes confusion. Put less on your slides. Fewer words and fewer bullets. Less is definitely more. Be very careful about embedded videos and/or too many effects. Simply because you can do it does not mean it helps the audience.

■ Brand power. Not every slide needs to have your logo, nor do they need to be in corporate colours. Too much brand power is a distraction.

Do use PowerPoint well. Go back to the original term: visual aid. A slide was meant to help the concept, not hinder it. Hence a PowerPoint slide is good for:

■ Graphs. Interesting stories and brilliant body language cannot replace a simple line graph if you are trying to explain growth in product sales. Graphs and pie charts can both be brilliant for explaining points, but keep it simple.

■ Pictures. What the new product will look like. Show it at the right time though – if the picture is ahead of your explanation, people will not be listening to you.

■ Schematics. 'This is our account management structure': show the structure of the department. Allow people to take it in by stopping talking, then perhaps take questions.

■ Quotation. 'Make a dent in the universe.' – Steve Jobs. Don't read the quote: they can do that.

■ Drama. A single number: 42. What's that about, they wonder? You can then explain.

Do present 'unplugged' more. Work on your:

■ State. Your state will create their state. Be enthusiastic and they will become so. Be boring and they will become bored.

■ Space. Don't stand behind a lectern: get out into the audience. Connect with them.

■ Story. Tell stories; people love them and remember them.

■ Structure. Get a logical flow which people can follow. A start, a middle and an end!

■ Spikes. Create change (a spike) to re-engage the drifting and wandering mind. A question, an activity, a story ...

■ Storyboard. You are a film director: plan your start, your ending, your car-chase!

■ Slides. Then, and only then, decide what slides you need. You'll find you won't need many, which is the way it should be.

Finally, present in this order:

■ Start with a wow – something to grab their attention e.g. the savings you are going to make for them;

■ Overview the structure of the presentation;

■ Talk about their needs;

■ Talk about your solution;

■ Take questions;

■ Summarise;

■ Close: ask for the order.

7. Use references and case studies

You have loads of references and case studies. You only need to ask and write them up. Do it and start quoting them!

8. Show you can do it by talking benefits

Facts don't sell. Benefits do. A benefit is what a fact means. Here are some facts: international company, available in red, cheap insurance. All well and good, but what do they mean? Any time you prepare or mention a fact, ask yourself '*So what?*' Only tell them that you are an international company if you can turn it into a benefit: '*Being international means wherever you are in the world and you want to run a campaign we can get it up and running for you within twenty-four hours.*'

9. Show them you can do it by being quantitative rather than qualitative

Facts can excite at the time, but when decision-makers leave the room they tend to remember only one. And it's a quantitative: price. So turn your qualitative facts into quantitative ones.

10. Show them you can do it by communicating in their style

Some people like big picture, some people like detail. Some people like to act, some people like to leave it for a couple of days. Work to their style. If people are comfortable, they're more likely to buy.

IN A RECESSION DON'T FORGET THE ABOVE, BUT DO FOCUS ON THESE ESSENTIAL FIVE

You need to keep progressing them to that obvious point: the point at which they buy.

1. Quantitative rather than qualitative

Anything which is measurable tends to get remembered. In a recession, you must make all of your special selling points measurable, i.e. quantitative. Thus, if you feel your service is extraordinary, your creativity wonderful, you must make those points measurable with facts and case studies.

2. Benefits and return on investment

Show the results you deliver and that you are an investment, not a cost. Prospects have a chance of arguing to invest, even in a recession, but they rarely want to add a cost when times are tough.

3. Reasons for action

In a recession, typically, anything which can be delayed, will be delayed. Show them why that is simply not a valid option for your solution. What exactly will they gain immediately? What exactly will they lose if the do not proceed?

4. Be truly engaging, don't just PowerPoint

Stand out and show your intelligence by working hard to understand their business and requirements, and showing exactly how you can provide a solution.

5. Be enthusiastic

There's a lot of gloom and doom around in recession. Don't be part if it.

EXAMPLES FOR BOOSTING BUSINESS IN THE RECESSION

At Inside-Out Gentleman's Tailor

Why not create a of book of tailoring examples, discreetly illustrating all price points? Make it less about history and heritage, and more about quality in a busy world.

At The Too Pink 'there's no glass ceiling' Consultancy

Why not scrap that big glossy brochure and create an exciting but minimalist study to which you attach a highly customer-focused covering letter?

At Intergalactic Software, EMEA Division

Why not ban the 'corporate slide-deck'? Remind people what selling really means and how PowerPoint is just a (small) component of that.

THE SURGERY IS OPEN

I take your point about customising the proposal, but sometimes we're just told to come in and pitch and if you don't like it, well, tough!

It's a tricky one. If we go in and do – effectively – a blind pitch, we are reducing our chances of beating the competition on strengths and we may only be able to beat them on price, which is not a situation we want to resort to too often. On the other hand if we stay resolute and say, '*Look, that's not what we do; we need a brief and the proper decision-makers*', they may say, '*Well, too bad then.*' Apart from a loss of face there's nothing to be lost by starting out asking for what you prefer: taking a proper brief. You're now selling them the benefits of giving you some time if they refuse. And you can still turn up to the 'show us your wares' show.

SUMMARY

■ Don't just show them you can meet their needs; convince them.

■ Convince them, so that their momentum doesn't evaporate once you leave the room.

■ Talk more benefits: what's in it for them?

■ Talk more measurable; how can they be confident it will work?

■ Talk more in their style; can they understand the benefits in their terms?

THINGS TO DO

1. Ban generic sales material, i.e. 'cut and paste' proposals, pitches, call plans. If they are generic they are – by definition – not selling. Just telling and hoping. Do this today.

2. Ensure all staff know how to turn generic brochures (which are of course there to get initial interest) into customer-focused conversations. Arrange the briefing.

3. Ensure the standard slide-deck does not exist, and eliminate the phrase 'Let's just pitch them the usual and see what sticks'. Today.

4. Train people how to present, not just show slides. Arrange a session.

5. Ensure they talk actions.

6. **Start today.**

7. Closing new business

● ●

WHY IS FORMALLY CLOSING NEW BUSINESS SO VITAL?

In more buoyant times, we can afford (literally) to be more relaxed about the definite confirmation of business and under what terms. A bit of a misunderstanding here, a bit of lost margin there, even a bit of business snapped up by the competition – well, it's part of life's rich fabric! Mmm … maybe. But we simply can't afford it in a recession. That's where the skill of closing comes into its own: we close to know we've got it. Or to know when we haven't got it and need to do something about it. But very importantly, it's never been the case that a 'magic close' can save bad selling; all good selling starts with the initial questions. And in a recession that's even more true.

WHAT YOU NEED TO KNOW: TEN REASONS AND WAYS TO CLOSE TO GET NEW BUSINESS

At any time of the economic cycle, rain or shine, these are the great whys and wherefores of closing to get new business.

1. Close to be sure

Never, ever assume you have got the business, until you have formally closed: *'So may I just check: you are happy with our proposal and you wish to proceed?', 'So how would you like to pay for the holiday, Sir? Credit card?', 'So is that a definite booking, Madam? Table for two tomorrow night at 7?'*

2. Close to know what to do next
If you are ever unsure of what to do next in a sale, close and work with the response: *'I've been talking a lot, is this all making sense?', 'So, no further questions?', 'Great, so can I take it we are all in agreement?'*

3. Close by simply enquiring
'I'm ringing you to find out if we've got the business.'

4. Close by giving alternatives
'Great, I'm pleased you're willing to see me. What would work better? Next Friday or the following Monday?' An alternative close is when both options are attractive to you; it is designed to make decision-making easier for the prospect.

5. Close by weighing up
'I agree. It can be hard to decide. What do you like about the competition?' Note what they say. Do not add to their list. Be neutral about the list; neither praise nor be rude about it. Then remind them what you offer. This latter list should be a lot longer if you (a) know your competitors and (b) have influenced well: *'So, like many business decisions it's not an absolute black and white decision but overall we do have far more strengths. Are you ready to proceed?'*

6. Keep closing

On small points and large points alike always keep closing: *'So are you happy with that as an agenda for the meeting? Great, let's start,'How would you like to pay: credit card or cash?'* Always be closing: ABC.

7. Close to start the negotiation

At some point they will start asking about discount. Avoid getting into this until you know they do want to buy, otherwise you are using discount to sell, the start of a slippery slope. (There's more on negotiation in Chapter 9, by the way.)

8. Close by following up

Always leave a call (face to face or telephone) with an agreed next action:*'Good, so I'll ring you next Wednesday around 3pm to see what's happened on the purchase order number.'*

9. Close by involving all the decision-makers

You can't close unless somebody can say 'yes'. Get all the decision-makers in the room: that's one reason we do presentations.

10. Just close

Ask. That's all it takes.

IN A RECESSION DON'T FORGET THE ABOVE, BUT DO FOCUS ON THESE ESSENTIAL THREE

When things get tough, your prospects will constantly be losing their confidence, their budget and their focus. You need to maintain all three for them by closing.

1. Keep closing and re-closing

Closing keeps you informed, closing keeps you up-to-date, closing stops you wasting your time and closing wins you the business. Consider it a feedback mechanism: *'Are you ready to go ahead with the pilot project?'* you ask (you've just closed, of course). They say, *'Sort of,'* to which you respond, *'And what's stopping that being a definite yes?'* They say, *'We have some concerns about your work in India,'* and you say, *'Let me go through that with you.'* When the issue has been resolved, you say, *'Are you ready to proceed now?'* and they say, *'Yes!'* (There's more on objection-handling in Chapter 8.)

2. Put more in writing

Take an extra five minutes to send them a confirmatory email covering the main points – it will save a lot of heartache later on.

3. Momentum

This is less of a technique and more of a mindset, a philosophy. Keep things moving. Bear in mind that every day, every pause could be a chance for the competition to act, for the market to get worse again and your client's confidence to disappear, for them to want to look at another supplier. So, keep it moving; always have a next action. Do not confuse this with being hassled nor rushed. We don't want to be rushed when choosing our meal, our suit or our holiday. When in conversation, be professional and patient. But then close and link to the next stage. Don't walk away and then ring up, that's exactly how momentum is lost.

EXAMPLES FOR BOOSTING BUSINESS IN THE RECESSION

At Inside-Out Gentleman's Tailor

When business has been finalised, suit provided, credit card accepted, why not ask, '*And when can we look forward to seeing you again? Shall I pencil that in the diary and give you a reminder call?*'

At The Too Pink 'there's no glass ceiling' Consultancy

Why not use the concept of ABC throughout your meetings to ensure you are on track and do not lose opportunities. Close on the agenda, close on small stuff, close on big stuff, close on the actions.

At Intergalactic Software, EMEA Division

Why not ensure all calls end with a proper close: a set of agreed actions. These are then summarised immediately in an email.

THE SURGERY IS OPEN

We like to think of ourselves more as consultants who don't do anything as brash as 'close the sale' Any views?

Where do I start?! Selling needn't be brash. Selling is nothing more than formalising much of normal conversation. If you're thinking of going to the cinema, you ask your friend whether she wants to go or not: you've just closed so that you can plan your evening. Closing isn't brash. Closing is what you do if you are professional. All jobs, teacher, call-centre leader, police officer, involve elements of selling. So do consultants. That's point 1! Point 2 is that if you do not close, you are likely to have wasted considerable time and energy, often to lose business to a competitor. If I were to be bold I would suggest that you seriously need to change your way of thinking or this recession could be the downfall of your consultancy. Is that brash enough for you?

SUMMARY

■ If you don't close you don't know whether you have won the business or lost the business or something in between, for sure.

■ In tough times, you need to know for sure.

■ Closing tells you exactly what to do next.

■ Closing is what brilliant sales people do. Consistently.

THINGS TO DO

1. Close more – today.

2. Close on more issues – today.

3. Close on more people – today.

4. Use more closing methods – today.

5. Put (perceived) agreements in writing – today.

6. **Start today.**

8. Handling objections

WHY IS HANDLING OBJECTIONS SO VITAL?

You're almost there. You've nearly got the credit card number and the official purchase order in your hand. And then: they have a worry. What happens if it doesn't work? What happens if it's late? What happens if the business goes bust, or the return isn't as good as you promised, or, or …? On the other hand maybe they want to delay: there's a new player in the market they'd like to consider. Perhaps they are simply messing you about, telling you they'd like more discount. All of these are what we might call objections. They may be real concerns, they may be sheer silliness or they might be negotiation ploys. Whatever is behind them they have got to be dealt with otherwise not only will you lose a sale, but you will have wasted a lot of your time.

Here is a key and powerful idea: an objection gives you your objective, in other words, it tells you exactly where to take the conversation next. Thus if they say they want more discount, you clearly have to (re-)convince them of the value of the solution. If they claim they want to hear what the competition has to say, you have to remind them of your USPs (unique selling points). Now you know the basics, read on for the detail.

WHAT YOU NEED TO KNOW: TEN TRICKY OBJECTIONS AND HOW TO HANDLE THEM

At any time of the economic cycle, rain or shine, these are potentially tough objections. Here's how to handle them.

Scenario 1: During the cold telephone call. You're ringing around to drum up some new appointments and you get the following objections.

1. I haven't got time

When people say they haven't got time, what they are really saying is that they don't want to think about it now. So make it easy for them. Here's a suggested response, '*Absolutely, of course you haven't got time, that's why I'd like to make an appointment. Is next week or the week after better for you?*'

2. Send me some information

The trouble is, once again, it's just to get rid of you. You'll waste your time and energy as they probably won't read it. How about saying, '*I could, but most of our current clients find it so much more helpful when we come to explain things face to face. When would be a good time to do that?*'

3. We don't have the budget

This objection should not come at a late part of the sale because if it does, it tells you that you failed to qualify. But if it comes when you are qualifying, what do you do? My suggestion is that if it is a company you would really like to do business with, you set up a meeting anyway, find out when they will have money and begin to influence their buying criteria: it's good to have some long-term prospects in the pipeline, too.

And remember, particularly with telephone cold calls, you must be willing to take a bit of rudeness. Stay polite and persistent, think long-term: if you can get an appointment you have a chance to do some real selling. You can handle a bit of rudeness if there's a chance to make a sale.

Scenario 2: At the boardroom close. You and your colleague have given a fantastic pitch but when you go to close the following objections come up.

4. We want to think about it

There are three possible stages to this. Stage 1, it is worth asking what aspect they want to think about. Maybe you will get an answer and be able to progress the sale. Stage 2, suggest you take 30 minutes out: often people simply need a bit of time to talk when you are not in the room, so go and sit in reception for a while and catch up on voicemail. That may free things up. Stage 3 is to agree the shortest timescale possible before you ring them back. Try later that day or first thing next day, certainly within twenty-four hours. Remember: the longer you leave them to think about it, the more worrying a sign that is.

5. We are still looking at the competition

Help your prospect to stop procrastinating. Use a flip-chart or white-board. Ask them for the points they like about the competion. Write the points down on one side of the board. Be neutral in your reaction to this list; do not comment and do not add to the list. Then list your points. Make sure this list is longer and contains plenty of USPs. Close by acknowledging that no business decisions are black and white, but point out that you believe you offer a much more complete solution.

6. We want some discount

Check that there is nothing else outstanding to be discussed. Then reiterate the value and list everything you are offering them. If they still want discount then read Chapter 9.

7. It's a bad time, there's a recession on

This objection requires that you not only stress the benefits of going ahead, but also point out the danger of not progressing. For example, *'I do understand that feeling, however what will happen if you do not continue to offer that option to your customer?'*

All of the elements below should form part of your general strategy.

8. Show empathy

In the majority of cases, it is perfectly understandable that someone has a concern. Your job is to reassure them.

9. Handle the objection

Answer the concern as best you can. Check that you have answered it fully and then ...

10. Close again

Now, just a brief point on getting a lot of objections. Perhaps you are trying to close a group, or you have a talkative person on the phone and either way there are four or five really key objections. A good strategy is to recognise that there are a lot of points to cover and say, '*You seem to have several points* (note the use of neutral language – 'point' rather than 'objection'), *let me write them down.*' Write all the points down. Ask if there are any others. Then answer them starting with the one you find hardest first, so that your responses only get stronger. Each time you answer one, return to the person who expressed it, check they are OK, then cross it out. Once all are crossed out: close again.

IN A RECESSION DON'T FORGET THE ABOVE, BUT DO FOCUS ON THESE ESSENTIAL THREE

When things get tough, there will simply be more objections.

1. Delay

Recession means constant delays while budgets get chopped and rationalised. Decision-makers get made redundant. New people come in and have to be convinced. There's no easy way round it but to keep qualifying, keep closing, keep handling the objections and your professionalism will on the day be rewarded with: a sale!

2. Shifting budgets

Keep qualifying. Do not be caught out.

3. Aggressive pricing

Companies still want stuff. In good times they get discount just to save money and just because they can. In bad times they are desperate. Keep reiterating your value, keep stressing your USPs. And if you must give discount (which we will discuss in Chapter 9), then keep it as small as you can.

EXAMPLES FOR BOOSTING BUSINESS IN THE RECESSION

At Mange-Tout Greengrocers

When they say, *'Oh, your cherries are dear!'* you respond, *'Absolutely, that's because they are so gorgeously sweet. Just buy a few less. They are well worth it. How many would you like?'*

At The Too Pink 'there's no glass ceiling' Consultancy

When they say, *'I'm not sure we want to deal with a consultancy which is so women-specific as we might miss out on the broader picture,'* you might say, *'We are a full consultancy; we simply specialise in the women's market.'*

At Intergalactic Software, EMEA Division

When they say, *'Intergalactic has a reputation for being arrogant,'* why not say (assuming it's true), *'Certainly we have recognised that our customer service has not been what we would have wanted in the past. But a recent initiative has completely changed that and we'd love to come and show you how different our approach is now: may we book a time?'*

THE SURGERY IS OPEN

The thing is it's often so difficult to think on your feet. The ideas above make perfect sense but in the heat of a call or a boardroom discussion it can be difficult to counter objections this smoothly.

I agree. And certainly in the first few years of our sales and marketing career, few of us get enough live practice at this essential skill. So you know what I am going to say: this is an essential skill to rehearse. When you pick up the phone, when you close your presentation, you should – mentally – have been there before. Arrange those training sessions!

SUMMARY

■ Summarise your main objections and practise how to handle them.

■ When you win or lose business be sure to review – with the client if at all possible – what helped or hindered the sale and in particular any objections you need to work on further.

THINGS TO DO

1. Update the pack of laminated index cards with key objections and their responses.

2. Schedule the first objection-handling training session.

3. **Start today**.

9. Negotiation

WHY IS THE NEGOTIATION SO VITAL?

Many of us find ourselves so grateful to be so close to – at last – getting a sale that we will do anything to get the business. She's almost bought the camera. They've nearly agreed to the twenty day consultancy deal. Nearly, almost, nearly. And we end up giving away our profit, or making agreements we simply can't really fulfil, or losing money on the sale, or possibly – even worse – accepting some business just to get cash, which distracts us from our core business. Yes, that final, final stage of the negotiation is pretty damn vital. Read on with care and note well.

WHAT YOU NEED TO KNOW: TEN ESSENTIAL NEGOTIATION TACTICS

At any time of the economic cycle, rain or shine, please do note these essential tactics. They'll save you money, profit and help you avoid sleepless nights.

1. Don't give unless you get

Once you have decided you are happy to give some discount, make sure it is with the condition that you get the business. Negotiation does not go like this:

Them: 'We'd like 5% discount.'

You: 'Well we don't usually, but OK.'

Them: 'Actually make that 10%.'

You: 'Alright, I want to get this moving.'

Them: 'How about 12%?'

But this:

Them: 'We'd like 5% discount.'

You: 'If I can get a purchase order number from you today, I'll give you 4%.'

2. Give small
A lot of negotiation is psychology. People like to feel they got another £10 off their purchase. Allow people to feel that they have won. Give small and build. If you know you could afford to give up to 12%, start with 3%.

3. Give odd
Discounts of 5%, 10%, 15%, etc., all make it seem as if it's just a game. When they ask for 10%, offer 3%, then maybe 7% or 8.5%. Odd percentages seem carefully calculated and therefore generate more powerful wins.

4. Give slowly

So, it takes you an extra 30 minutes to get a good deal. That's fine. You'll be living with the consequences of this agreement for some time, maybe years.

5. Do the calculations

Before you go into a negotiation and if necessary during the negotiation: do the calculations. Let's keep it simple. You sell for £100. Your cost is £50. So that's £50 profit? Lovely. But now you give 5% discount. Assuming your costs are fixed (we're keeping it simple), you've just given away 10% of your profit. Mmm, something think about.

6. It's often not about price

It's because the person you are talking to has got to tell their boss they got a deal. Help them with that. But maybe you can offer a service which doesn't erode profit so much.

7. Check the terms and conditions, especially payment terms

Keep reviewing the whole picture. So they want 12% and they only want to pay you in 90 days. No way. Maybe the negotiation is a chance to change something. So perhaps offer 12%, but insist on 45 days payment terms.

8. New year, new contract

Back to zero: one terrible assumption which buyers love to make is that whatever discount they get in one deal will be rolled over into another deal. Ensure that all negotiations are locked into one deal or one contract or one financial year and are not universal.

9. Do an amazing job

When the negotiation is over, whether you are pleased with the result or not: do an amazing job. Then you'll have the upper hand next time. Now they really know how good you are.

10. Close again

Remember: it ain't over until it's signed and sealed.

IN A RECESSION DON'T FORGET THE ABOVE, BUT DO FOCUS ON THESE ESSENTIAL THREE

When things get tough, we can no longer rely on people coming to us or the light-touch ways of getting business. We need to get tougher, more proactive and more focused.

1. Protect your profit

Calculate, calculate, calculate. Understand the cost of every concession, every point of discount, every free offer of postage and packing, every free tie offered with a shirt. Arithmetic – in this instance – is power.

2. Check all the terms and conditions

Keep looking at the big picture. What else are they expecting of you? Are they assuming anything they shouldn't?

3. Believe in yourself
Develop personal resilience; remember that companies still want stuff. In good times they get discount just to save money and just because they can. In bad times they are desperate. Keep reiterating your value, keep stressing your USPs. And if you must give discount then negotiate properly.

EXAMPLES FOR BOOSTING BUSINESS IN THE RECESSION

At Mange-Tout Greengrocers
Why not offer those who spend over a certain sum with you a 'carry to car' service on your quiet days? This encourages customers to spend more and use a resource which is available anyway on quiet days.

At The Too Pink 'there's no glass ceiling' Consultancy
Why not offer some extra discount in exchange for some of the work they usually offer to other consultancies? After all, they know how good you are, don't they?

At Intergalactic Software, EMEA Division
Why not refuse discount but offer a place or two on one of your training courses? Then they'll discover how good that service is and buy more training from you.

THE SURGERY IS OPEN
But we are in a market where the buyer has all the power. If we resist their demands for huge concessions won't there always be someone else?

You know, here's an interesting thing: everybody says that about their market! Everybody! Whatever market you are in: wine for supermarkets, consulting for IT companies, window-cleaning to local councils, these buyers all need a decent product. They have to get a decent product whether it is toilet rolls or air-conditioning systems. So that's the first thing to stress and prove (as we have detailed in the last few chapters): sell your value. Sell your USPs. Remember how often we have stressed, good selling is all done early on in the sales cycle; you must have sold, they must want you.

So here's an important truth: if you can only get business by selling on price, you need to improve your offering. Once you have a decent offering, practise saying 'no' more often and offering less discount more often and you will notice it does work. If you don't get this right, you'll be out of business; and that's no fun.

SUMMARY

- Believe in your company, your product and you: sell their combined value.

- Negotiation is as much a game of psychology as a real desire for a lower price.

- Play the game; put the time in.

- Don't give away your profit.

■ If you do have to give away profit, know exactly how much it is costing you.

THINGS TO DO

1. Update the pack of laminated index cards you produced for your team with the rules of negotiation:

    ■ Check you have sold before you start negotiating;
    ■ Don't give unless you get;
    ■ Give small;
    ■ Give odd;
    ■ Give slowly;
    ■ It doesn't have to be about price;
    ■ Keep closing and checking what you have agreed;
    ■ New contract/new financial year: back to zero.

2. Ensure everyone gets regular negotiation training.

3. **Start today.**

10. Account management

● ●

WHY IS MANAGING THE ACCOUNT SO VITAL?

There are many things which are frightening about managing a business in a recession. A major one is the lack of predictability. When will the phone ring? When will we get more orders? When will we win some business at decent profit? In better times, there's a steady stream of enquiries which turn into business. But in a recession this is unlikely to be the case. In the gloom, though, there is a glimmer of light: your regular accounts, your steady customers. We all have them in some form or another: they buy from us every month, we do their windows every morning. If we manage these clients well they can give us the element of stability which we so desperately need. After all, if they have been a regular, surely they must value us? So whatever money they do have why would not they spend it with us? Good point, so here's how to make that more of a certainty.

WHAT YOU NEED TO KNOW: TEN WAYS TO MANAGE THOSE ALL-IMPORTANT REGULAR ACCOUNTS

At any time of the economic cycle, rain or shine, these are the great whys and wherefores of getting business from your regular accounts:

1. Never assume

Don't think that they can't go elsewhere. OK, your support is great and there is an awful lot of their time and energy invested in the relationship with you. But never assume they can't go elsewhere. Always give them the best treatment. Keep reminding and showing them what is special and unique about you.

2. Stay in close touch

As we fight for new business to close the gap between what is coming in and what we need to survive and/or keep the bank manager away, we can so easily take our eye off the ball of who pays most of the wages. Have regular meetings with your account, whether or not they are spending. Even if an account goes across to the competition: stay in touch. You want to know when they are ready to buy again. Never lose touch with someone who has bought from you: if they were a customer once, they can be a customer again.

3. Make sure they really know what you do

They may not know your full range of products. Tell them the full story and make sure all your contacts in the account know fully what you do.

4. Always have something new to say

Tell them about new product developments and case studies. Do not allow 'account management' meetings to become just boring rituals. Offer value through your ideas and conversation, even if you can't sell them your product, yet.

5. Ask for leads and introductions

Ask for introductions to new decision-makers in the business. Ask to be introduced to more senior people in the business. Ask for introductions to people they know in other divisions, other businesses and, if appropriate, even other industries. Everybody knows somebody. And you want to talk to that somebody.

6. Do a brilliant job, especially with the 'soft' side

If you are dire, you'll be out of the account, and that will happen pretty well immediately. There is no long term if dire is your chosen standard. If you are poor, it may take a little longer for the account to catch up with you, but you'll be out once they realise and once again there is no long term for you. If you choose to be OK, then you can often survive for a while if business is buoyant; but in a recession there's no way. You simply can't stay at OK! Who wants to buy from someone who is OK? They will wish to choose from someone who is good, someone who is very good.

If you are good, then the account should be moderately pleased with you both short term and long term. Will you be able to hang onto contracts? No – that's right: probably not. You see, good is no longer good enough. Certainly not in the long term, not in a recession. But hopefully if you are good you are good enough to recognise the need to raise your standards. How about if you are very good? Ah, now we're talking. Accounts are delighted with you. There are more possibilities open to you. You should have more choice over your business direction; you should get regular consideration for some of the best opportunities.

What about if you are excellent? Wonderful. There are never, ever enough excellent businesses about the place. You'll be in demand, you'll always be employable. Could you step up to outstanding? Of course you could. Because you've got the message, haven't you? Every one of these steps is a choice. Your talent is genetic, but your standards are choice. And if you were outstanding, think of what would be open to you. And if you were awesome there would be absolutely no stopping you. How about it? Simply decide to be awesome. They'll be after you. You can name your price.

7. Ask specific questions about new budgets and next year's plans

Plan ahead. What are the new projects? When do the budgets come on line? Keep steering the agenda to put your company in the best light.

8. Learn avidly about the account

In the end, you are a money-making machine. If you can make money and in particular profit for your account then they will keep you engaged. But to make them money you need to understand how they make money themselves: ask questions. Become an expert.

9. Ensure every account has an account manager

He or she will be responsible for that account: no excuses, no surprises. They know it as if they worked there.

10. Ensure every account has a plan

Make the plan simple. Decide what you want to achieve in the account and how you are going to do it. Break down the latter into action, owner and date. Easy!

IN A RECESSION DON'T FORGET THE ABOVE, BUT DO FOCUS ON THESE ESSENTIAL THREE

When things get tough, your accounts will want to switch off spending, and when they do spend, they will feel they are entitled to special deals. And remember that the offers that are held out to them by the competition will be very tempting. Here's what to do.

1. Keep re-iterating the value and in particular the USPs you offer

Great discounted deals are very, very tempting of course. You must make completely explicit what you offer so that the account is clear on the possible damage to their own business if they are no longer working with you. Sell the relationship, sell the soft stuff. Make intangibles tangible. Make implicit explicit. Make qualitative quantitative.

2. Stay close

You know your account. So no news is not good news. Unreturned calls or ignored emails should ring alarm bells: act, before it's too late.

3. Stay strong

Believe in yourself and remember that a good account will know what you do for them and will talk a lot about going elsewhere to weaken your negotiating position. Believe in yourself: acknowledge their concerns but remind them – once again – of what you do for them.

EXAMPLES FOR BOOSTING BUSINESS IN THE RECESSION

At Inside-Out Gentleman's Tailor

Why not set up a simply loyalty process for all of your regulars to dissuade them from buying from another outfitters?

At The Too Pink 'there's no glass ceiling' Consultancy

Why not write to every single one of your accounts (active or not) asking them to email you ideas on how you can improve your support? If any don't reply, ring them up. Just that simple process will flush out some business anyway.

At Intergalactic Software, EMEA Division

Why not make sure every account has an owner who is passionate about developing an ever better relationship between Intergalactic and the account?

THE SURGERY IS OPEN

Many of our accounts are telling us that in tough economic times we are simply too expensive. How do we stop them going to the competition?

Let's assume for the moment that you are not really 'too expensive', but it's the usual issue that you are perceived to be too expensive and also the competition are doing some amazing deals to get into your accounts. (If you really are too expensive, you have a fundamental problem beyond our remit here. You need to reconfigure your marketing strategy: try *Instant MBA*, for some real, rapid help.) No, let's assume it's those two interconnected factors: familiarity has caused them to assume they're not getting the best deal any more and the competition are a-wooing. Here's a plan:

1. Ensure you are doing a great job in the account. Familiarity can cause a lack of attention to detail. Ensure excellence is being delivered.

2. Remind the account of all you do and all that is included. A lot of the things you do are not on an invoice. Ensure the account realises and appreciates this before they move to the competition and then realise too late for them and too late for you.

3. When doing pricing debates try these points:

   ■ 'Are we comparing like for like? OK, sure, their training is bundled and therefore sort of 'free' but they do charge for cabling which we do not.'
   ■ What about the running costs? Anybody can create a cheap 'up-front' deal to win the business, but what about over the

length of the life of the product? What is the cost of not being able to get rapid, professional support, for example?
■ What about all the details such as payment terms, volume discounts?

4. If the competitor really is cheaper, ask your client whether they think the competion can really afford to do that for long, as you don't see it (presumably) as a viable business model.

5. If none of the above does the job, you need to make a decision. You can drop the account – a tricky one to make, as the cost of sale of finding new business is colossal. Or you could be pragmatic and say you will match the price for, say, six months while times are hard. Of course only do this if you see the account as being one which can be a winner for you long term and if you can afford to service them with the new lower pricing model.

SUMMARY

■ Your accounts are the bedrock of your survival.

■ Your accounts are the foundation of your growth plans.

■ Ensure every account has a plan and an owner.

■ Prioritise accounts for appropriate time and attention.

THINGS TO DO

1. Assign an account manager to each of your important accounts.

2. Ask them to produce a plan for the account.

3. Review that plan at least every two weeks.

4. Identify the necessary actions and implement them.

5. Assign time to an account by potential pay-off, not just by current business generated nor by 'niceness' of your contact.

6. **Start today.**

11. Personal resilience

● ●

WHY IS PERSONAL RESILIENCE SO VITAL?

In those heady days of a buoyant economy when you were reading management and sales books you may well have come across the advice to 'work smarter, not harder' and in such times it's good advice. The reality is that in recessionary times you still need to work smarter: that's what 98% of this book is about, specifically for the sales and marketing skill-set. But you'll need to put the work in, too. But let's be absolutely clear: by that we don't necessarily mean long hours. What we do mean is absolute focus and attention.

This is because nothing you want, whether it's increased sales or more profit, will happen unless you give it that incredible focus, that dedicated attention. To do that you'll need to be tough, you'll need to be resilient. So will your team.

WHAT YOU NEED TO KNOW: TEN WAYS TO MAINTAIN YOUR PERSONAL RESILIENCE, ENERGY AND FOCUS

At any time of the economic cycle, rain or shine, these are the essentials for being the best version of you.

Get more focus with the following ideas.

1. Know what focus is

During tough times, meet regularly as a team and decide what it is you are after, what it is you are going to focus on. Have three time frames: the next twenty-four hours, this week and this month. Then get that on the white-board, on your screensaver. Do whatever works for you. Focus. Support that by – and this is absolutely vital if you are a leader of people – getting your own quiet, reflective time. All you need is paper and pencil: what are the issues, what do we need to focus on?

2. Minimise trivia

Don't spread your business or yourself too broad. Be wary of deals which seem good and do get some cash in, but take you well away from your core business. Get rid of customers who simply aren't worth it because of all the time and resources they drain. Sort out the terms and conditions if customers are confused about a support issue and you spend ages after the sale sorting it out. Outsource your book-keeping if doing the VAT is not your speciality and the time to relearn it every three months and sort out the mistakes could be spent more valuably elsewhere.

3. Take proper breaks

Every forty-five minutes: stretch and sip water. At lunchtime take a break of forty-five minutes away from your phone and keyboard. Include some walking. Go home and have a decent evening. You know that there is always more to be done, so you might as well stop while you are still fit rather than work yourself into a stupor.

4. Boost your productivity
These lower productivity (paradoxically):

- Meetings. Reduce them by at least 50%, and when you do have meetings, insist on a purpose, a timeline and agreed actions.

- Skipping lunch. It'll save you forty minutes now, but lose you hours in lowered energy mid-afternoon and spoil your evening because of loss of 'spark'.

- Aiming for instant email zero. No email is so critical. Batch process, check your email at regular but well-spaced intervals. In between: do some work!

- Command and control leadership. It's a sure fire way to lose the best from people.

- Chain-drinking coffee. Choose coffee for pleasure, never for energy. It doesn't provide the latter.

- Working at home evenings and weekends 'to get on top of stuff'. You never will. Prioritise and zone.

- Believing that productivity is getting stuff done. Wrong, productivity is getting the right stuff done.

These boost productivity (paradoxically):

■ Freeing space in your diary. Block out some time to use your thinking: your reflective intelligence.

■ Going high-touch. Sometimes, all you need is pencil and paper; listening to understand; being there for a person.

■ Using the phone, again. The phone carries all the necessary emotions and nuances, even if it's just voicemail.

■ Leaving at half past five. You have a life. If that life is enriched you will have energy for the next day.

■ Saying no. When you say yes to more work you say no to Lego on the floor with your daughter.

■ Taking a walk. Too easy? Try it.

■ Looking at the night sky on a clear night. And saying wow at the top of your voice. So, the neighbours know you are weird. Don't worry about it.

Get more energy by following these ideas.

5. Walk more
Walk at lunchtime. Walk to the railway station. Build in simple cardiovascular exercise every day.

6. Eat properly

Don't skip meals. Reduce 'grabbed' junk food eaten in the car at speed. It's not good for your health and it's terrible for your driving.

7. Reduce the energy drainers

Poorly run meetings, badly set up email systems, long drives along motorways. Invest a little bit of time in improving the way you do things to make the future so much easier.

Reduce stress by trying these ideas.

8. Adjust your thinking

It's either a lost deal or a chance to learn how not to do it that way next time. Choose your perception. Here are some useful ones:

- No failure, only feedback. OK, so the account management meeting went dreadfully. Why and how can we ensure it never happens again?

- Love the dip, love the plateau. Improvements rarely go in nice easy steps. Cold calling. Presenting. Negotiation. They are all challenging but as long as the overall path is onwards and upwards – that's fine.

9. Spend time away from work

Really switch off the BlackBerry. Yes you can: it's good for you, it's good for your relationship, it's good for your children. And actually it's good for your creativity – and hence your business – as your brain is finally getting a chance to process rather than just receive. Spend time with friends and family. Book time away and mark it in your diary. Yes, I know there is a recession on. But one day, boom time will be back. There will always be a reason to defer. Do it now: your health, your family, your kids … your guitar playing, your Italian lessons depend on you spending some time away from work. It'll make you a better salesperson or marketer, too.

10. Keep in mind the bigger picture

This is a tough time, but it will be over. You are clearly preparing yourself much more than many. There is business to be had out there. You can pull through and be an even fitter business.

IN A RECESSION DON'T FORGET THE ABOVE, BUT DO FOCUS ON THESE ESSENTIAL THREE

When things get tough, you need to get tougher.

1. Super-focus

Be absolutely clear what business you do want in this recession and what you don't. Ensure all activity matches to that purpose.

2. Stay well

Take time out to stay well. That's not just so that you don't have to take any sick days but also so that you make creative decisions and are able to inspire the team.

3. Keep an eye on the team
Check that they are copying your good practices of taking breaks and going home on time. All you require of them is brilliance when they are at work! That's more likely if they have a home life.

EXAMPLES FOR BOOSTING BUSINESS IN THE RECESSION

At Inside-Out Gentleman's Tailor
Why not take your lunch break? Radical, I know, but you'll be more energised in the afternoon – it could just work!

At The Too Pink 'there's no glass ceiling' Consultancy
Why not encourage every consultant to set up regular four-day weekends where they totally forget work and come back refreshed?

At Intergalactic Software, EMEA Division
Why not introduce simply yoga classes at lunch times and at the end of the day?

THE SURGERY IS OPEN
I'm just hyped. I can't relax. I just think, or more realistically, worry, about work all the time. I wake up at four in the morning worrying about whether we actually posted the full proposal. Even when we close business, I can't enjoy it, I'm worrying about where the next bit of work will come from. How can I learn to take a break from work?

You are not alone. Here are some ideas:

- Zone, in other words, return home to being a sanctuary. Don't take work home.

- Decide when you will leave work, and leave work at that time.

- Eat properly during the day: eating large meals in the evenings is not good for quality sleep.

- Return the bedroom to a sanctuary. Stop it being a home office and give up the bad habit of sitting in bed doing email.

- Wind down several hours before bed. Start reading novels again.

- Certainly ensure you exercise (simply walking is fine) during the day.

- Seriously consider taking up a stress management approach such as meditation or yoga.

- Remember that when you are stressed you will not want to do any of the above as you feel you do not have enough time, but you must if you are serious about your health and your business.

SUMMARY

■ Your wellness is essential to you being the best version of you.

■ The survival of your business or career depends on you being the best version of you.

■ There are four elements to your wellness: relaxation, exercise, diet and sleep. Attend to each, fully.

■ Remember that when your body is unwell, it's often a simple feedback system suggesting you slow down and give yourself some time and space.

THINGS TO DO

1. Take exercise: just simple walking and taking the stairs will do as a start.

2. Sleep fully and well.

3. Eat properly: more nutritious food and less junk.

4. Relax properly: no email from, say, seven o'clock at night until six o'clock the next morning.

5. Encourage your team to follow similar behaviours.

6. **Start today**.

12. Leading the team

● ●

WHY IS LEADING THE TEAM SO VITAL?

It's challenging enough keeping *yourself* energised, resilient and focused, but there's a whole extra dimension to consider when you are leading a team of sales or marketing professionals too. The thing about a team is, it's fantastic if it really is a team with everybody supporting their colleagues; the team collectively knows what it's doing and has a positive buzz. But if the team is actually a collection of individuals then not only have you got a challenging external environment – i.e. the economic downturn – to deal with but you also have internal politics causing friction and lowered performance. You need a high performance sales and marketing team, and here's how to create one.

WHAT YOU NEED TO KNOW: TEN WAYS TO CREATE A HIGH PERFORMANCE SALES AND MARKETING TEAM

At any time of the economic cycle, rain or shine, here's how to get that team to buzz. Get more focus by following the tips below.

1. Give them a clear, collective purpose

They can't be a team (beyond their title anyway) if they don't have a reason for needing each other. The best way to create that co-operative need is through the process of exchanging best practices and ideas, e.g. discussing how to handle objections, exchanging slide-decks of great pitches, briefing each other on possible market opportunities. Get them talking at team sessions. And obviously *have* team sessions.

2. Catch them doing things right

Catch individuals doings things right and they will feel better about themselves. Catch the team doing things right and it will encourage them to work as a team. Time and time again, it has been shown that once the hygiene factors (e.g. a desk, a chair, a computer) have been sorted, it is feeling valued, it is feeling one is growing, it is being part of a great team which will get the best out of a person. You are the facilitator of that process.

3. Give them growth and stretch opportunities

Give each salesperson a chance to succeed. Ask them for examples to lead the team meeting or to attend a high-level negotiation with you. Anything which gives them growth opportunities.

4. Give them a chance to understand one another

It's difficult to dislike somebody if you've really got to know them. Give your team a chance to do that. Create some social time. It's not lost time; done well it will be paid back several times in the office.

5. Model excellence

Who's good at what? Get them to share their skills.

6. Institute team training sessions

Set up and run training on all the skills we've been talking about in this handbook: as a team.

7. Insist on honest, open feedback

One of the reasons for getting the team to know each other socially is they can then talk to each other honestly and directly about challenges they might face with each other.

8. Work hard, play hard and respect difference

Expect hard work. Give opportunities to play. But remember not everyone wants to go to the pub, not everybody can get to team pizza. Be inclusive with team ideas.

9. Model the behaviours you seek

If you want your team to listen to you and to each other, then listen to them. If you want your team to turn up to training, go on it yourself.

10. Walk your talk

Stop talking about what you will do, do it.

IN A RECESSION DON'T FORGET THE ABOVE, BUT DO FOCUS ON THESE ESSENTIAL THREE

When things get tough, 'team power' is critical. The collective spirit can pull though one individual's bad day. Create team power by keeping these three ideas in mind.

1. Catch people doing things right

Recessions tend to give an individual a real feeling that things are just not working out, that despite all the work they are putting in, they are simply not getting results. It is vital that you remind them that things are working, they are making progress and they are valued.

2. Connect one to one

Ensure you sit down one to one with each member of your team at regular intervals. Connect and understand what makes each person tick.

3. Celebrate success

As a team, use every excuse to announce good news and celebrate.

EXAMPLES FOR BOOSTING BUSINESS IN THE RECESSION

At Inside-Out Gentleman's Tailor

Why not have a team off-site workshop and get some industry experts in to talk to you about what's happening in tailoring?

At The Too Pink 'there's no glass ceiling' Consultancy

Why not book regular one to ones with every one of your consultants?

At Intergalactic Software, EMEA Division

Why not instigate sales breakthrough of the month? Small or large, it (and the creator) gets celebrated.

THE SURGERY IS OPEN

But what do I do about the non- or underperformers?

The same as you would any time. Identify the non/underperformance. Discuss it with the individual and agree a plan to close the gap: provide training or coaching as necessary. A recession is fascinating in one sense: it really brings out the best in some people as they rise to the challenge. Unfortunately, it also reveals that one or two have been coasting and hiding behind buoyant business. Be firm but fair. Identify the issue, discuss it and ask for change. And if it isn't working seek advice from your human resources team or external professional adviser.

SUMMARY

■ Your team is more important than ever during a recession both to you and to each team member.

■ A properly functioning team can have more energy, more focus, be smarter and still have more fun. And boy are all of those needed in tough economic times.

THINGS TO DO

1.   Book team meetings.

2.   Book some team socials.

3.   Book one to ones.

4.   Actively 'catch people doing things right'.

5.   **Start today.**

13. The A to Z of selling in a recession

● ●

Read, learn and memorise. Photocopy this A to Z and put it onto your index cards. Put copies up around the sales office. Test the team. Live and breathe the A to Z of selling in a recession.

A IS FOR ACCOUNT MANAGEMENT

Love your accounts. Once you have won business, work hard to turn them from one-off customers to regular clients and then into profitable accounts. Never, ever take them for granted nor assume they are locked-in to you. Look after them: sell to them as you would to a brand new exciting prospect. Your regular accounts help you sleep at night, they establish your credibility as references and they help you forecast your growth. They are more vital than ever in a recession where the cost of getting new business is huge and the cost of losing an established accounts is catastrophic.

Act!

■ Who's in the decision-making unit of each of your accounts?

■ Have you made contact with each of them in the last five working days?

■ Are you quantifying the value you are offering?

■ Have you asked for references and leads to help you sell elsewhere?

■ What's the next action in each of your accounts?

B IS FOR BLOCKER

Every day of the recession, of every account, ask: who or what are the potential blockers in this sale or account? How – in our worst nightmares – could we lose this business? How will you handle them? Is it lack of money? Is the key decision-maker too weak? Is it your lack of knowledge? What needs to be done? Do it, sort it, resolve it: now!

Act!

■ Who could block us?

■ What could block us?

■ How can I resolve/anticipate that?

C IS FOR CLOSING

Every day, every meeting: always be closing. Don't leave it until some big finale. Close every stage, every agreement. It's not a social conversation. This is a professional business conversation. Close it all down: get the who, where, when and why. They should all be in no doubt. You should have no doubt. In a recession, never ever assume anything. Close more frequently, with more people. ABC: always be closing.

Act!

■ Close by asking: *'So are you ready to…?'*

■ Close by using dates: *'So when…?'*

■ Close by using alternatives and options: *'So, which…?'*

■ Just close.

D IS FOR DECISION-MAKING UNIT (DMU)

There will rarely be a single decision-maker, especially in larger or more complex sales. Decide to track down each element of the DMU and ensure that they are happy. Don't let one or more of them appear at the last stage and block your sale. Remember that in a recession, the power base can change even more quickly, people can be made redundant. Keep asking, 'Who decides?'

Act!

■ Who's the strategic (big picture) DM?

■ Who's the financial DM? Are they cost or return on investment?

■ Who's your champion?

■ Who's the user?

■ Who's the technical DM?

E IS FOR ENTHUSIASM

Do you possess energy and enthusiasm? Are you in great shape? Because sales are made both logically and emotionally. Have you addressed the emotional side? Do people *want* to do business with you? In a recession they have too many choices. Ensure they want to work with you; if all else is equal maybe this will be the one factor. Invest in the relationship by ensuring you never let them down, do what you say you are going to do and have great energy.

Act!

Make sure you are in the best possible state for any meeting or presentation:

■ Sleep well;

■ Eat well;

■ Exercise well;

■ Relax well.

F IS FOR FEAR

Fear blossoms in a recession. Will it ever get better? Will we ever get any business again? Feel the fear and do it anyway (said Susan Jeffers). Work the skills in this book and do the major presentation, the cold call, the meeting with the CEO, the objection-handling board meeting, explaining your return on investment calculations: live. They will all get easier and you will start getting results.

Act!

■ Decide what your fears in the sales arena are.

■ Prioritise them (greatest fear first).

■ Work on them and eliminate them, one by one.

G IS FOR GOAL

Never take the next step in the recession without a clear goal. What do want? Survival? Sure. But there will be a time after this downturn. What kind of customer do you want long term? You cannot afford to waste time. Having a goal will ensure you are least likely to do that. Have a goal when you make a phone call, a visit, send a proposal, write an email, make a presentation. Ask yourself: what am I trying to achieve?

Act!

■ Set a goal.

■ Ensure it is measurable.

■ Ensure it has a time-frame.

■ Ensure it is realistic.

H IS FOR HEAR

Recessions are not a good time to make assumptions: that's when we lose the business. Forget that 'I've heard it all from the client a million times before' attitude and really listen. Listen and hear what they say and what they want and why they want it and what their concerns and worries are and who they are still attracted to in the competition. If you listen, if you really hear what they say, then you'll have all you need to excel at selling. But if you hear only what you want to hear you are stuck.

Act!

■ Take key not verbatim notes.

■ Regularly 'play back' for accuracy and confirmation.

I IS FOR INSIDER

Develop your internal 'moles'. Those who keep you informed, who warn you of politics. You need an insider, a friend, a coach.

Act!

■ Think about who is really helping you get the facts on money and time-scales.

■ Work out who's ensuring that there is consistency across stories.

J IS FOR JUMP!

In a recession make sure you jump higher than your competitors. Offer the highest standards of service. Not just good, not just very good, not just excellent, not even outstanding, but awesome. *Don't* sell on price, sell on your ability to jump higher than anyone else.

Act!

■ Deliver what you promise at least.

■ Deliver more than you promise, often.

■ Delight the customer every time.

■ Aim for awesome.

■ Boy, will they remember and recommend you.

K IS FOR KILLER APPLICATION

What will absolutely wow them? What are your unique differentiators, your incredible case studies, your mind-blowing financial return stories? What is special about you? How can you really, really show that you are an investment not a cost, even in a recession?

Act!

Ensure you have your:

■ Best case studies;

■ Best stories;

■ Best financial argumentation;

■ Best references.

L IS FOR LEARN

In a recession, learn and get feedback. Keep noticing what's working. What messages get your customer to buy? What helps defend price? Learn, learn, learn. Decide in one year's time not just to be better than you are now, but, say, 15% better.

Act!

■ Read more.

■ Attend more courses.

■ Review your own performance after selling.

M IS FOR MONEY

The problem with the recession is money. It always was important. Now it's the number one thing to your customer. Make sure it is for you, too. It's all about money, really. Their money: how much have they got, and how much can you make for them? It's about your money. How much will you make: in this sale and over the lifetime of the customer relationship? You need to know how much they have got and who controls it. Thinking money helps you prioritise. How are you making them money (business to business) or saving them money or leaving them more budget to buy more clothes (business to consumer)?

Act!

■ Turn qualitative into quantitative.

■ Talk profit.

■ Talk return on investment.

■ Think margin.

N IS FOR NICHE

In this recession what's your area of specialty? Develop it quickly. As a consequence, you will be even more effective. As a consequence, you will win more business. As a consequence, you will earn more money. Do you have any:

■ Strengths?

■ Weaker areas?

■ Areas you want to develop?

O IS FOR OBJECTIONS

Everybody always wants to know how to handle objections such as 'it's too expensive,' 'it's not the colour we were after' or 'we have budget restrictions'. Don't think of it as a technique, instead stay natural. Start by turning the objection into an objective. If they say that it seems too expensive, your objective is to give them a better understanding of the value of the product or service you offer. Once you know what the objective is, you clearly know what to do next.

■ Expect objections.

■ Remember that objections seek clarification.

■ Understand that objections are buying signals.

P IS FOR PROSPECTING

In the recession, it is vital that you keep the 'funnel' full. What ratio of calls and other enquiries become prospects? Which become customers? Which become clients? Which become advocates? Know your ratios. Perhaps develop a points system. Aim to hit a certain number of points per day.

■ Suspect = 1 point.

■ Prospect = 2.

■ Customer = 4.

■ Client = 8.

■ Advocate = 16.

Q IS FOR QUESTIONS

What do you need to know? So what are your questions? You certainly need to know what they want. What would cause them to choose you, who will make the decision, how do they make decisions and who else are they looking at? So get to it: ask questions. Do it skillfully, though; this is not an interrogation but a professional consultative business conversation

■ Ask about money.

■ Ask about the decision-making process.

■ Ask about their needs.

■ Ask open questions.

■ Ask closed questions.

■ Ask niche questions, and ask now.

R IS FOR RAPPORT

If they don't trust you, if they don't like you, then it doesn't matter how magical your product and argumentation is – they'll always feel wary. Build trust. Do what you say you are going to do. Give them attention. Never assume.

Act!

■ Meet your promises.

■ Give them 100% attention.

S IS FOR SELL

Too much selling revolves around qualitative information coupled with relationship building. While valid, you will stand out from the crowd when you build your differentiator, you will create you argumentation when you increase your quantitative side. This becomes critical in a recession when it is very much about giving the customer the confidence to buy. Provide:

■ Sound qualitative statements;

■ Sound quantitative statements;

■ Sound relationship building.

T IS FOR TODAY

What action can you take today to further 'lock in' and build value in each of your accounts? Who can you call? Who can you email? What sales book can you read? What presentation can you sharpen up?

Act!

■ Make a call.

■ Write a note.

■ Learn some product information.

■ Map out an account.

■ Develop a white paper.

■ Read some trade information.

U IS FOR UP

Sell 'up'. You can't sell strategic investment unless you talking to the people who understand that kind of thinking and language: so find them! Lock into the account at higher and higher levels of decision-making. Keep asking for introductions to increasingly more senior people. Learn how to talk their strategic language and what they need to know.

Act!

■ Be of strategic value.

■ Be a business partner.

■ Work as a professional.

V IS FOR VALUE

In a recession, everyone wants to talk price. Let them do that but don't be drawn in. Sell value and sell results. Stay away from pure price as an argument, because you cannot win long term. Of course you might win some short-term business, but what happens next time? Absolutely, they'll want an even better discount.

Act!

■ Explain what results you offer.

■ Draw attention to what makes you unique.

■ Let them see how you quantify your results.

■ Encourage them to calculate the benefits of doing work with you.

■ Get them to work out the cost of not doing work with you.

W IS FOR WHO

Who can help you? Who can help you develop your skills, find new prospects, expand the account, further your career? Develop your network: this is so important in a recession. Tap every possible route, build your personal network, spend time with the best people. Ensure that you invest in relationships: don't always expect an immediate return.

Act!

■ Develop your network.

■ Record your network whether it be in a rolodex, a diary or a database.

X IS FOR XS

Yes, okay, we cheated a bit here. What we're talking about is excess. Business is really, really tough in a recession. But don't pursue it to excess; know when to turn away, when to move on, when to decide an account is not profitable. Know when to look after yourself, to take a break or go for a walk, to go home, to watch a film, to play with your kids.

Act!

■ Walk away, sometimes.

■ Say no, sometimes.

■ Take a walk, a lot.

■ Leave the email and get some sleep more often.

■ Start now!

Y IS FOR YEAR-END

What really counts in a recession is the end-point. Perhaps it is the quarter, perhaps it is the year-end. It's not really about your Power-Point slides, nor about whether you got your expenses in on time. Whatever: are you focusing on the ultimate target? What will you bring in? Where is it coming from? Are you certain? What would increase your certainty?

Act!

■ Create a prospect matrix: prospect amount by month expected.

■ Identify three sources of new business.

Z IS FOR ZEN AND THE ART OF SELLING

Love selling: it's an art form as much as a science. A recession gives you a chance to really show how good you are. Anyone can sell when times are good, when business is buoyant. Don't let anyone be dismissive of the skill you are developing: we all sell, all of the time. Decide to be brilliant at it. Read to learn more. Listen to learn more. Do to learn more.

Act!

■ Selling is an art. Treat it as such.

■ Develop your portfolio of skills and knowledge.

■ Read.

■ Listen.

■ Learn.

14. Helping business come to you: brilliant at the basics marketing

● ●

If you hadn't realised before, you'll certainly understand by now that the big, big difference in a recession is you have to **sell**. Much of the low-key marketing activity in buoyant times is simply insufficient to get people to your door. Having said that, can you put a definite tick against every one of these (mostly budget) marketing ideas?

1. You have a web-site. It's up-to-date, and it's really easy to find your telephone number and email on it. But above all it is quick to load: get rid of all that fancy Flash stuff, straightaway.

2. You have a simple brochure. It is available in both paper and electronic format. It's up-to-date. It sells rather than tells. When a request is made for either (especially paper) it goes out instantly.

Don't respond to a prospect with second class mail. What's that telling them?

3. All emails sent out have a proper sign-off and change on a regular basis to promote a product of yours. The sign-off contains your direct dial and mobile number.

4. Everybody who answers the phone is incredibly helpful and don't sound as if they have been disturbed from something far more important than serving the customer.

5. You constantly feed stories to the local press. The local press is desperate for column inches and some of your prospects and customers do read it.

6. You keep the key vertical market press in your field up-to-date even though they ignore you. Your day will come, and they can't do anything if they don't hear from you.

7. You don't do blanket mailings, paper or electronic. You are very choosy. You work out who you really want to do business with and target them with carefully produced mailers.

8. You are bold. Have courage. Don't be a sheep. You don't have to attend an exhibition simply because everybody else does. If it's not getting you great business, do something else with your time and money.

9. You've got smart business cards with large type and easy to read numbers. Use the back to sell.

10. If you are sending an important proposal by post, send it registered. And phone to check it has been received.

11. You work your network. That's business associates, customers and clients. It's also friends and family. Return the favour and help them out.

12. Anybody who rings and is a brand new prospect or customer gets asked how they heard about you. You maximise and replicate methods which seem to work.

13. All sales materials talk benefits, i.e. what a given feature means to your reader, the customer.

14. You've worked out your ratios and what works so that you can turn up the flow of suspect to prospect to customer to client to advocate.

15. You try everything at least once. For example, PR: if you've never tried it, why not? Maybe it's perfect for you.

16. Reception is, well, receptive.

17. You are happy to get specialist help: find a trusted expert at running exhibitions, for example.

18. Meeting rooms are pleasant to be in. Boxes are in box rooms. Stale coffee cups are in the kitchen. Cables are tucked away.

19. You have a database of customers: keep it up-to-date and stay in touch with everyone on it.

20. All enquiries are logged and tracked: to the bitter end.

21. You are constantly asking yourself who talks to the people you want to talk to but isn't a competitor, and could you exchange ideas with them? You sell water-coolers, they sell coffee. It seems like a perfect match.

22. You think Kotler: price, product, place, promotion, and never assume anything.

23. Why are your prices what they are? Cost-based? Perception-based? History? Five per cent less than the competition? Five per cent more than the competition? Start experimenting with price. The first place to start is working out if any of your products have great price elasticity. In other words, can you up the price without demand dropping, or if it does drop is the change so small as to make the increase still well worth doing?

24. Your product. Are you really listening to your customers; could you be leading your customers? Remember, nobody *needed* an iPod.

25. Your place or channel. Could you sell via other channels? The obvious one is online. Could you get rid of an unprofitable channel of two?

26. Back to promotion. How do you promote your product? Test every method available to you. Cost-justify products/services against each other and ensure you have the best mix for you.

27. You are always reading a marketing book. Start with *Instant MBA*. If you've read it already, brilliant, now start working your way through its reading list. Marketing isn't about mail shots. It's about brilliant actionable ideas which build your business.

15. Brilliant at the basics: boosting business at your business

● ●

Any business can boost its selling success by getting brilliant at the basics. Try writing a list of ten things off the top of your head for your company. Here are five business examples to get you started. Get your team to do it at meetings, and get all of your employees to do it at the annual conference!

TEN WAYS TO BOOST BUSINESS AT YOUR CLOTHES SHOP

1. Open on time, not late.

2. Concentrate on the customer, not your first beverage of the day.

3. Display the clothes so their potential in outfits is seen rather than single discrete components.

4. Ask open questions rather than closed questions: 'How may I help?' rather than 'Can I help?'

5. Make sure the changing rooms have ample room for changing.

6. Make the regulars feel special.

7. Make newcomers know they can easily become regulars.

8. Think about the mood the music is creating: is it want you want?

9. Resist constant discount sales.

10. Make friendly contact with every customer.

TEN WAYS TO BOOST BUSINESS AT YOUR BISTRO RESTAURANT

1. It may be French, Spanish, Italian or even Portuguese. But give it a name we can say without sounding foolish.

2. Less is more. Do a few things well. Great (short) wine list. Great (short) dessert list.

3. What do people come to you for? Romance? Family ambiance? Choose which and maintain this.

4. Light the candles on time.

5. Replace the menu cards before they are dirty.

6. Get clear on your tipping policy. Ensure the bill can be read in candlelight.

7. Allow people to sit where they want, not where you want just so you can fill the window.

8. Be attentive but not fussy.

9. Never, ever use less than the best ingredients.

10. Thank people for coming.

TEN WAYS TO BOOST BUSINESS AT YOUR COFFEE SHOP

1. Open on time, not late.

2. Get better pastries if you know yours are too dry.

3. Clear the tables of unappetising dirty cups, quickly.

4. Offer free wi-fi.

5. Smile.

6. Make a perfect espresso, the heart of all your drinks.

7. Make sure the menu is easy to understand and simple to order from.

8. If you are going to do it, do it well. If you offer milkshakes make sure they are as good as your coffees.

9. Make sure the customer toilets are clean at all times.

10. Ask your trusted regulars for feedback.

TEN WAYS TO BOOST BUSINESS AT YOUR AIRLINE

1. Tell us – honestly – what is going on.

2. Set up all lines early and clearly and fairly.

3. Sort out your security system. Shoes on or off? Laptops in or out?

4. Help people whose travel plans are messed up as a result of your delays.

5. Treat people nicely even though they booked economy seats.

6. Fix the coffee so it tastes great.

7. Don't charge for water.

8. Ensure the entertainment system works.

9. Tell us – honestly – what is going on.

10. Oh, for goodness' sake, tell us what is going on.

TEN WAYS TO BOOST BUSINESS AT YOUR DELICATESSEN

1. Think about your systems. What happens if we just want coffee-to-go?

2. Open on time.

3. Make sure everything looks clean, fresh and the best of best. Your sundried tomatoes my be superb but they won't look it displayed in a cheap plastic bowl.

4. Help us to learn about the cheeses, meats and exotic produce you offer. If we know more, we'll buy more.

5. Be green as soon as you can be. What about offering recycled, reusable bags?

6. Ask people how they heard about you and use that method to spread the word.

7. Change the window display regularly.

8. Help us tell others; give us a card.

9. Have a cheese or chutney of the day to get us curious.

10. Be friendly.

Now it's your turn!

16. You've got to be different

Selling and marketing in a recession is so much easier if you are different. It gets people to come to you and only you, it helps you defend your price and it makes it easier to create publicity. Read this list then decide how you you'll become even more different.

A BEGINNER'S GUIDE TO DIFFERENCE – 101 GREAT IDEAS TO GET YOU THINKING

1. Apple does it by being cool.

2. Steve Jobs knows form is function.

3. iPod or Zune? It's a no-brainer.

4. The *Guardian* does it by quantity and quality and speed to its online market.

5. You can do it by price: but only for the 17 nanoseconds before somebody undercuts you.

6. You can do it by a clever feature but only until somebody copies you.

7. Do it by service: faster, friendlier, easier.

8. Do it by experience: longer-lasting. More colourful.

9. The local window-cleaner does it by giving out his home phone number to clients.

10. Difference can be friendliness like Innocent Drinks.

11. Bloggers create difference with their free ideas.

12. The Beatles did it by constant reinvention.

13. Don Winslow does it by tight action-paced writing with fantastic characters.

14. How are you different?

15. What's your brand?

16. Your brand is what people say about you when you are not present.

17. You don't want to be like some brands. Dull. Dreary. So what?

18. You want to be the Grand Central Station, New York of your field.

19. So, how are you different?

20. It could be your standards.

21. Dire is a standard – the kind that gets you sacked.

22. Poor is standard. That gets you sacked, too.

23. OK is a standard. Until the first reorganisation.

24. Good is a standard until the second reorganisation. Good is no longer good enough.

25. Very good is a standard which gets you noticed.

26. Excellent is a standard which gets you opportunities.

27. Outstanding is a standard which gets you chased.

28. Awesome is a standard which gets you the world.

29. Audi does it by consistency throughout its range.

30. Volvo now does it by safety-desirability.

31. Bose does it by amazing sound quality.

32. The local primary school did it by banning junk food during the day.

33. You do it by insisting your meetings run on time, to time.

34. Singapore does it by being clean. Everywhere.

35. New York does it by being exciting.

36. Be different by caving in less to price pressure.

37. Position yourself as special.

38. Get *them* to choose *you*.

39. You'll survive the recession through difference.

40. The Rolling Stones do it by being the 'Greatest Rock 'n Roll Band on the Planet' – even though they say it themselves.

41. It's much more fun to lead than to follow – a great reason for being different.

42. If you're different you'll thrive in the recession.

43. Be different by being longer-lasting.

44. Why not go back to old-fashioned vanilla flavour?

45. Could you do it in red?

46. Is being local your USP?

47. Is it time to expand your presence online?

48. Are you friendlier than the competition?

49. Perhaps you're cooler.

50. Maybe you're more knowledgeable.

51. Try *not* using PowerPoint.

52. Try seeing people rather than sending an email.

53. How about being on time?

54. Don't forget to be courteous.

55. Lufthansa does it at Munich airport by making it so easy to check in.

56. Mercury does it by being a liquid metal.

57. Difference means you are special.

58. They'll choose you *because* you're different.

59. If you're different they'll want you.

60. Most video rental companies don't do difference – but one could.

61. Most banks don't do it – but one could.

62. Most shops don't do it – but could.

63. The Body Shop used to have it with no animal testing.

64. 'In times past you could be obscure but secure – now that's harder.' Michael Goldharber, *Wired*.

65. Cirque du Soleil has it by reinventing theatre.

66. Phaidon Press does it by design.

67. Singapore Airlines does it by being courteous, even in economy class.

68. It's not the product.

69. It's the brand – a bit.

70. It's certainly the service.

71. Mostly it's the experience.

72. Experience is about investing in the customer.

73. It's not that the customer is always right.

74. It's not that customers know what they want.

75. Customers *are* your life-blood, though.

76. Decide to be different.

77. Organise an off-site workshop or away day.

78. Ask, 'How are we different?'

79. Decide how you can be more different.

80. You're either distinct or you're extinct.

81. 'There is very little difference in people, but that little difference makes a big difference! The little difference is attitude. The big difference is whether it is positive or negative.' Dale Carnegie

82. Kotler's 4Ps could help: **P**rice, **P**lace/channel, **P**romotion, **P**roduct.

83. Upgrade your skills constantly.

84. Difference is a choice.

85. Difference is a mindset.

86. Difference can be sheer energy.

87. Difference can be sheer oomph.

88. Difference can be on the road thirty minutes earlier.

89. How are you different?

90. What's your brand?

91. Your brand is what people say about you when you are not present.

92. So, how are you D.I.F.F.E.R.E.N.T.?

93. D – distinct

94. I – inspirational

95. F – focused

96. F – fearless

97. E – energised

98. R – ready-to-go

99. E – entrepreneurial

100. N – niche targeted

101. T – top of the field

10. Perhaps your cabling price per metre could be increased by 3%. It doesn't sound like much, but over time and over bigger projects you'll notice the difference. And remember it's not a discretionary purchase, so they will need to buy this.

11. All this attention on the here and now is great. But are you making long-term progress, too? And what long-term thinking needs to be done?

12. Think about that account you would *love* to have. Who's going to do the cold call? That'll be you, then!

13. When's the next 'let's go (not too) wild' session? You have to have some fun, you know. Fix a date, let everyone know and make sure it's fully inclusive, not just free beer for the lads.

14. Is there anyone with whom you can partner to 'increase the pie' for both of you?

15. Maybe you sell water for water-coolers. They sell coffee for coffee machines. Can you sell into each others customers? Of course you can.

16. Re-analyse what your potential customers do, read and eat. What would be a simpler or cheaper way to speak to them? What about an advert in the flower bed at the junction to the industrial park where they all seem to be based? They don't allow ads? Surely you can overcome that objection!

17. What needs do you meet? How can you make that need more acute? Bigger? More urgent? Needed by more people? Anybody will buy anything as long as they have a big enough why.

18. Who's your best salesperson? How much better are they than your weakest? What do they do that makes them better? Transfer that skill or attitude across the rest of the team – **now**.

19. When's the first training session? Still not booked. Come on!

20. Read and reread this book. Ask the sales team to read handy tips at the sales meeting. If an idea is agreed to be valuable, implement it – don't just talk about it. Get hold of my books *Beat the Recession* and *Instant MBA*. I mean it – I believe in my products!

21. Who buys from you? Which are your key accounts? How do you thank them? Do they know you love them dearly? It's no good telling them when they leave you.

22. Drink more water. Take a five-minute break every 45 minutes. Take a lunch break of 45 minutes.

23. Go home on time.

24. Thank people for doing a great job.

25. Keep in mind what is really important: don't get trivia hypnosis.

18. Resources

● ●

Here at Infinite Ideas we have a wealth of resources to help you, especially in tough times.

For more background on many of the ideas in this book, consider *Instant MBA: Think, perform and earn like a top business-school graduate.*

To help you with people-influencing issues, read *Have it Your Way: 52 brilliant ideas for getting everything you want.*

If you're feeling isolated in business and need to make some useful contacts try the ideas in *Networking: Work your contacts to supercharge your career.*

Some valuable ideas for leading, motivating and communicating with your team can be found in *The Living Leader: Become the leader you want to be* and specific ways to motivate your sales team are thoroughly covered in *Turn Your Sales Force into Profit Heroes: Secrets for unlocking your team's inner strength.*

Sun Tzu's *The Art of War: A 52 brilliant ideas interpretation* will provide you with some great tips on strategies for business, while Napoleon Hill's *Think and Grow Rich: A 52 brilliant ideas interpretation* will help you work out how to consolidate your position in business and keep your finances healthy.

If you need to take a look at your business from a new angle and work out some inspired solutions to your business problems, take a look at *Unleash Your Creativity: 52 brilliant ideas for creative genius*.

Three books that could help promote your business to new customers and get your web-site really working for you are *Web-sites that Work: Secrets from winning web-sites, Get into Bed with Google: Top ranking search optimisation techniques* and *Google AdWords that Work: 7 secrets for cashing in with the world's no.1 search engine*.

On a more personal note try *Sort Out Your Money: The only book you need to get you through the recession*, which is full of ideas on how to thrive rather than merely survive at work, at home and at play during the recession.

Oh, and if it all seems to be getting on top of you, take some time out with *Stress Proof Your Life: 52 brilliant ideas for taking control* and learn some techniques for keeping your head in these tricky times.

19. 100-word story

• •

His neighbour said he didn't think he'd be working beyond the week. The guy at the petrol station was in a really low mood. The local Starbucks was quieter than usual and the usually sunny barista Anne-Marie wanted to know whether he knew when it was all going to end. He didn't. He parked his car in the underground carpark and jogged up the three flights into the office. He turned off the alarm, switched on the lights, got the coffee brewing and prepared for the 8.30 Monday morning meeting. His theme: **Let's sell our way out of this recession.**

Thanks for reading this book. Good luck and stay in touch at www.nicholasbate.typepad.com

Index